AF577115

Basket-Work of the North American Aborigines

Extract From: Smithsonian Annual Report 1884. Vol. 2

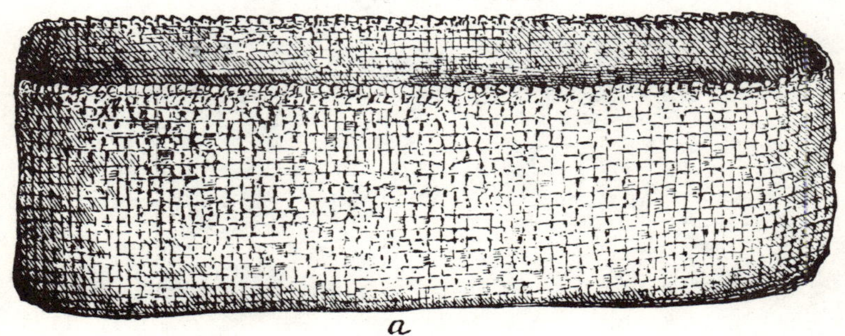
a

by Otis T. Mason

Facsimile Reproduction 1968
THE SHOREY BOOK STORE
815 Third Avenue
Seattle, Washington 98104

SJI #5

THIRD EDITION FACSIMILE REPRINT
LIMITED TO 250 COPIES

AUGUST 1973

ISBN #0-8466-4005-8

II.—BASKET-WORK OF THE NORTH AMERICAN ABORIGINES.

By Otis T. Mason.

"Barbara de pictis veni *bascauda* Britannis,
Sed me jam mavult dicere Roma suum."
—Martial, xiv, 99.

The study of the minutest technique in the distribution of aboriginal arts is very necessary in making up our opinions on questions of Anthropology. The archæologist is frequently caused to halt in the reconstruction of ancient society by his ignorance of the arts of the savages around him. This is especially true of an art which had its culmination in savagery or barbarism, and which began to decline at the touch of civilization, or at least to give place to higher types of the same art. For the discussions of problems that have arisen in the past the data then in hand have been sufficient; but as the investigations of social progress become more intricate the demands for greater detail in the observation of anthropological phenomena around us is imperative.

I have lately had occasion to examine all the baskets in the National Museum, and the results of this research may not be uninteresting as a contribution to exact technology in an art which may be called *par excellence* a savage art.

In a basket there are several characteristics to be observed, which will enable us to make a classification of the objects themselves and to refer them to their several tribal manufacturers. These characteristics are the *material*, the *frame-work*, the *methods of weaving*, the *coiling or sewing*, the *decoration*, their *use*, &c.

The tool almost universally used in their manufacture is a bone awl or pricker and the makers are the women. Of the manipulation of the material previously to the weaving little is known.

In the drawings accompanying this paper the actual size of the specimens is indicated by a series of inch marks in the margin. The inches on the standard line are shown by spaces between dots. In order to indicate exactly the manner of weaving, a square, usually an inch in dimension, is taken from a portion of the surface wherein all the methods of manipulation occur. This square inch is enlarged sufficiently to make the structure comprehensible. This plan enables us to show form and ornamentation in the whole figure as well as the method of treatment in the enlarged inch.

ALEUTIAN ISLANDS.

Mr. William H. Dall has contributed to the National Museum a large number of Aleut grass wallets, conoidal in form when filled (Fig. 1). The warp is of coarse straws, radiating from the center of the bottom. The covering or woof is made by plaiting or twisting two straws in a coil or twine, crossing them between each pair of warp straws. It is as if a twine of two strands had a straw or osier passed down through every half turn (Fig. 2). This plait or twine may be driven close home so as to be absolutely water-tight, or the weaver may leave spaces from one twine to the next wide enough to make a net. A very pretty effect is produced by these Aleutian basket-weavers by splitting the warp straws and twining woof straws around two of the half straws, joining 1 by 2, 3 by 4, 5 by 6, at one round, and the next twine inclosing 0 by 1, 2 by 3, 4 by 5, and so on. This produces a series of lozenge openings (Fig. 2). The split warp strands are often crossed to form X-shaped openings, or carried straight so as to produce parallelograms. I have observed the same effect in Peruvian mummy cloth, but a greater variety of network is there produced by alternating the rectangular and lozenge meshes in bands varying in width.

In the "Smithsonian Contributions to Knowledge," No. 318, plate 7, Mr. Dall figures and describes the matting of the Aleutian Islanders found in the caves in the Catherina Archipelago.

The method of manipulation in the matting is the same as that just described for the basketry of the Aleuts, and the delicacy of workmanship is most admirable. This method of weaving by means of twining two woof strands around a series of warp strands occurs in many places, and will hereafter in this paper receive the name of "twined basketry."

In a covered basket made of split bamboo from the Malabar coast the fastening off at the top of the basket and the weaving of the cover have a three-stranded twine. At every third of a turn the splint that is inward is hooked or passed behind the warp splint at that point. This produces a very smooth effect on the inside and a rough surface without.

The mats of the Aleuts are made of the fiber of the *Elymus** treated as hemp. The ornamentation on the outside of the mats and baskets is formed by embroidering on the surface with strips of the straw instead of the macerated fiber which forms the body of the fabric. The embroidery stitches in these, as in most savage basketry, does not always pass through the fabric, but are more frequently whipped on, the stitches passing always between the two woof strands, as in aresene embroidery, showing only on the outside. Mr. Dall justly praises the marvelous nicety of this Aleutian grass-weaving, both in mats and basketry.

There is no Chinese or Japanese basket in the National Museum showing this plaited weft. The grass of these Aleutian wallets is exceed-

* *Elymus mollis*, Sitka, Norton Sound, Kotzebue Sound; *E. arenarius*, Norton Sound, to Point Barrow; *E. Sibiricus*, Sitka. (See Rothrock, Smithsonian Report, 1867.)

ingly fine, the plaiting done with exquisite care, the stitches being often as fine as 20 to the inch, and frequently bits of colored worsted are embroidered around the upper portion, giving a pleasing effect. The borders are braided in open work from the ends left in the weaving, as follows (Fig. 1):

At some point on the border, when the solid part of the wallet is finished, the weaver bends two warp strands in opposite directions and gives each a twist with its next neighbor. These two are braided with the next warp thread; these three with the next. Now, start at a proper distance from the first point of departure and braid both ways, as before. These braids will meet and form a set of scallops around the edge, fastened at the ends and loose in the middle. Also, at the apex of each scallop will be a lot of warp straws, braided indeed at the base but loose for any required length. The weaver commences with any set of these to make a four-ply braid, catching up the next set and braiding them in as she went along, and fastening off a set as each new set is taken up. The upper border is thus a continuous braid, connected at regular intervals with the apices of the braided scallops. When the braider reaches her starting point she catches one braid into another, in a rather clumsy manner, and continues to braid a long four-ply string, which, carried in and out the scallops, forms a drawing-string.

ALASKAN ESKIMO.—Two types of baskets are found in close proximity in the neighborhood of Norton Sound—the twined and the coiled. In the former (Fig. 3) the treatment is precisely the same as in those of Aleutian Islands, but the Eskimo wallet is of coarser material and the plaiting is a little more rudely done.

The basketry of this type, however, is very strong, and useful for holding food, weapons, implements of all kinds, and various other articles. When not in use, the wallets can be folded up into a small space like a grocer's paper bag (Fig. 3). In the bottoms of the wallets of this class the weft is very open, leaving spaces at least one-half inch wide uncovered. The borders are produced by braiding four strands of sea grass into the extremities of the warp strands.

Ornamentation is produced by darning or whipping one or more rows of colored grass after the body is formed—not necessarily after the whole basket is completed, for each row of whipping may be put on just after the row of coil on which it is based (Fig. 4). Another plan of attaching the ornamentation is very ingenious but not uncommon. Two strands of colored straw or grass are twined just as in the body of the basket, and at every half turn one of the strands is hooked under a stitch on the body of the basket by a kind of aresene work. This ornament has a bold relief effect on the outside and is not seen at all on the inside.

The coiled variety of the Eskimo basketry, mentioned above (Fig. 5), consists of a uniform bunch of grass sewed in a continuous coil by a whip stitch over the bunch of grass and through just a few bits of grass in the coil just beneath, the stitch looping under a stitch of the lower coil. When this work is carefully done, as among the Indians of New Mexico, Arizona, and California, and in some exquisite examples in bamboo from Siam and in palm-leaf from Nubia, the most beautiful results are reached; but the Eskimo basket-maker does not prepare her coils evenly, sews carelessly, passing the threads sometimes through the stitches just below and sometimes between them, and does not work her stitches home (Fig. 6). Most of these baskets in the collection of E. W. Nelson have a round bit of leather in the bottom to start upon (Fig. 5, *b*). The shape is either that of the uncovered band-box or of the ginger-jar. Especial attention should be paid to this form of stitching, as it occurs again in widely-distant regions in a great variety of material and with modifications producing striking effects.

The association of this coiled form of basket-making with the marks on the most primitive types of pottery-making has been frequently noticed by archæologists. It is also well known that the modern savages of our Southwest build up their pottery in this manner, either allowing the coils to remain or carefully obliterating them by rubbing, first with a wet paddle of wood, and afterwards, when the vessel is dry, with a very fine-grained stone.

The Eskimo women employ in basket-making a needle made of a bird bone ground to a point on a stone (Fig. 100). Fine tufts of reindeer hair, taken from between the hoofs, are extensively used in ornamentation, especially in the Aleutian area.

TINNÉ INDIANS.

A few specimens of basketry from the vast Athapascan area contiguous to the Eskimo belong to the coiled type (Fig. 7). Instead of a bunch of grass, however, a rod of willow or spruce root is carried around in a coil and whipped on with a continuous splint of similar material (Fig. 8). The stitches of the coil in process of formation, passing regularly between those just below and locking into them, alternate with them and give a somewhat twilled effect to the surface* (Fig. 8). If now a strip of bast or grass be laid on the top of the osier or spruce root coil and carried around with it, and the sewing pass always over these two and down between the bast and the osier of the coil below, a much closer ribbed effect will be produced. Several specimens of this kind of coiled basketry, in which a strip of tough material is laid on top of the coiled osier, were collected at the mouth of the Mackenzie River by McFarlane and Ross, and Mr. Murdoch has shown me a basket similarly wrought, from Point Barrow, which he thinks many have been obtained by barter from the Tinné Indians in the vicinity. The ornamentation on one specimen of this type is very

*The working of this stitch is described and figured by Paul Schumacher in XII Report of Peabody Museum, p. 524: the coils are not, however, interlocked in all cases; that is, if the foundation rods were pulled out the stitches would separate and the whole structure come apart in some cases.

curious and elaborate (Fig. 9). The basket-maker had a number of little loops of bark and quill of different color prepared, and every time a stitch was about to be taken the lower end of one of these loops was caught over the splint thread and held down. The next stitch fastened the two ends of the loops home (that is, each stitch caught the lower part of a new loop and fastened down both ends of the preceding one after it had been doubled back), giving a series of imbrications (Fig. 10). On this specimen are between 3,000 and 4,000 separate loops sewed. This is one of the most striking examples of savage patience and skill, and must have occupied in its construction many hours of a renowned artist.

Mr. Jones tells us, in the Smithsonian Report (1856, p. 323), that the Hong Kutchin Indians, who live on the headwaters of the Yukon River, make basket-kettles of tamarack roots woven very neatly and ornamented with hair and dyed porcupine quills. The water is boiled by means of hot stones thrown in. For dyeing the roots and quills they use berries and a kind of grass growing in the swamps.

In looking at these coiled baskets, standing geographically so far removed from the Apache and Navajo country, one is reminded that the migration which separated these branches of a great stock may have been northward and not southward, and that the Tinné may have carried with them the art of making coiled baskets learned in a region where its beauty culminates.

CHILKAHT INDIANS.

The basket work of these Indians is superb. Every one who sees it is struck with its perfection of workmanship, shape, and ornamentation. All the specimens of the National Museum collection are of the band-box shape; but they can be doubled up flat like a grocer's bag (Fig. 11). The material is the young and tough root of the spruce, split, and used either in the native color or dyed brown or black. The structure belongs to the twined or plaited type before mentioned, and there is such uniformity and delicacy in the warp and woof that a water-tight vessel is produced with very thin walls. In size the wallets vary from a diminutive trinket basket to a capacity of more than a bushel. All sorts of lovely designs in bands, crosses, rhombs, chevrons, triangles, and grecques are produced thus: First, the bottom is woven plain in the color of the material. Then in the building up of the basket bands of plain color, red and black, are woven into the structure, having the same color on both sides. Afterwards little squares or other plain figures are sewed on in aresene, that is, only half way through, giving the most varied effect on the outside, while the inside shows only the plain colors and the red and black bands. The wild wheat straws are used in this second operation, whipped over and over along the outer threads of the underlying woof, or two straws are twined around in the manner explained above (page 293, bottom).

No more attractive form and ornamentation of basketry are to be seen than those produced by the Indians of this Thlinket stock extending from Mount Saint Elias to Queen Charlotte Archipelago, including Sitka.

HAIDA INDIANS.

These Indians live on Queen Charlotte Archipelago and adjacent islands. Their basket work differs in form from that of the Chilkahts, or Thlinkets, owing probably to the demands of trade; but the twined method is followed (Fig. 12) and the ornamentation is produced in a similar manner. The quality of the ware, however, is a little degenerated and more gaudy (Fig. 15). The Haidas are very skillful in imitating all sorts of chinaware in basketry, such as teapots, sugar bowls, toilet articles, table mats, bottles, and hats. They also introduce curved lines and spirals with good effect. The basketry hats of spruce roots, the most striking of their original designs, are made by the twining process (Fig. 14). The crown is twined weaving of the most regular workmanship and the fabric is perfectly water-tight when thoroughly wet (Fig. 15). An element of ornamentation is introduced into the brims by which a series of diamond patterns cover the whole surface (Fig. 16). This decoration is produced thus: Beginning at a certain point the weaver includes two warp strands in a half twist, instead of one; then makes two regular twists around single-warp strands. The next time she comes around she repeats the process, but her double stitch is one in advance of or behind its predecessor. A twilled effect of any shape may be thus produced, and rhombs, triangulated fillets, and chevrons made to appear on either surface.

The "fastening off" of the work is done either by bending down the free ends of the warp and shoving them out of sight under the stitches of the twisted web, or a braid of four strands forms the last row (Fig. 16), set on so that the whole braid shows outside and only one row of strands shows inside. The ends of the warp splints are then cropped close to the braid. This appearance of the entire four-stranded braid on the external surface is produced by passing each of the four strands alternately behind one of the warp sticks as the braiding is being done (Fig. 16). (Compare this with what was previously said about the basket from the Malabar coast, page 292.)

Special attention should be paid to the painted ornamentation on these hats (Figs. 14 and 15) showing head, wings, feet, and tail of the duck, laid on in black and red in the conventional manner of ornamentation in vogue among the Haidas and used in the reproduction of their various totems on all of their houses, wood and slate carvings, and the ornamentation of their implements.*

*A very interesting instance of survival is to be seen in the rag carpets of these Indians. The missionaries have taught the women to save up their rags and to cover their floors with pretty mats. They are allowed to weave them in their own way, however, and the result is a mat constructed on the ancient twined model, precisely as the weaving is done on the mats and hats.

The method of manufacture of Haida twined basketry is shown by Mr. J. G. Swan in a specimen collected expressly for the National Museum (Figs. 17–19). Mr. Swan says, "This style of making baskets differs from that of Cape Flattery. There the women sit on the ground and weave baskets and mats, both of which rest on the ground."

With the Haidas the mats are suspended on a frame and the baskets supported on a stick as in Fig. 17. The black color of the spruce root used in making ornamental patterns is produced by soaking it in the mud. Fig. 18 shows the bottom of the basket made by the twining process. The border of the bottom is marked off by a row of double weaving or a twine built outside the body of the basket just as in the Eskimo basket before described (page 293). A section of the structure is shown in Fig. 19 where the border ends.

BILHOOLAS, ETC.

Along the coast of British Columbia the great cedar (*Thuja gigantea*) grows in the greatest abundance, and its bast furnishes a textile material of the greatest value. Here in the use of this pliable material the savages seem for the first time to have thought of checker-weaving (Fig. 20). Numerous mats, wallets, and rectangular baskets are produced by the plainest crossing of alternate strands varying in width from a millimeter to an inch (Fig. 21). Ornamentation is effected both by introducing different-colored strands and by varying the width of the warp or the woof threads. In several examples the bottom of the basket is bordered with one or more lines of the twined or plaited style of weaving, to give greater stability to the form. Cedar mats of great size and made with the greatest care enter as extensively into the daily life of the Indians of this vicinity as do the buffalo robes into that of the Dakota Indians. They may be seen upon the floors, sleeping berths, before the doors of the houses, and they are also used as sails for their boats and wrapped around the dead.

It is not astonishing that a material so easily worked should have found its way so extensively in the industries of this stock of Indians. Neither should we wonder that the checker pattern in weaving should first appear on the west coast among the only peoples possessing a material eminently adapted to this form of manipulation. It is only another example of that beautiful harmony between man and nature which delights the anthropologist at every step of his journey.

MAKAHS AND CHIHALIS.

We are now introduced to still another style of basketry, very primitive but capable of very delicate treatment. I do not know of its existence outside of the Nutka stock living on the southwest side of Vancouver Island and on the northwest corner of Washington Territory, except in two cases, to be presently mentioned. It may be called the "fish-trap style," since without doubt the finer basketry is the lineal descendant of the rude wicker fish-trap. Imagine a number of stakes driven into the ground pretty close together. A horizontal pole is laid against them in the rear, and by the wrappings of a withe around the pole and each upright stake diagonally on the outside and vertically on the inside, a spiral fastening is produced (Fig. 23). This stitch crosses the two fundamentals in front at an angle and the horizontal frame-piece in the rear at right angles, or *vice versa*, and the lacing may always run in the same direction, or the alternate rows of lacing may run in opposite directions, as in Fig. 23. As a matter of fact, in soft and pliable material this operation constantly pushes the uprights forward a little, giving to the fabric an appearance of the back of a watch (Figs. 24–26).

The Clallam Indians of the Selish stock make a carrying basket in this manner (Figs. 22, 23), the frame (warp and woof) sticks being about one-eighth inch in diameter, lashed in place with split ozier or root. The Japanese also make a fish-trap similarly, with the exception that the coiled splint passes alternately backward and forward, so that if the horizontal were pulled out the fabric would tumble to pieces. The oblong oval shields of bamboo, made by the Bateke negroes of the Lower Congo, imitate this structure exactly. The frame of the shield is an oblong hoop on which are stretched splints of rattan, running longitudinally on one side and transversely on the other, crossing at right angles except at the plano-convex space at the ends. Splints of bamboo, about one-eighth inch wide, are woven into these cross strands precisely after the manner of the Makah basketry, the consequence being a series of square stitches on the back and diagonal stitches on the front, closely fitting, and coving the surface completely. Now, if the frame were cedar-bark threads about the size of pack threads, and the lashing of white sea-grass, we would have the Makah basket (Figs. 24–26). It takes three sets of threads (Fig. 25), the radiated warp, the coiled woof, and the spiral-binding thread, to finish the compound. No other area is known to the writer where this peculiar pattern is wrought into delicate fabrics. The Makahs belong to the Nutka stock, most of which are on the southwest shore of Vancouver Island, including the great group of Aht tribes. No Aht basketry is in the Museum, but it would be extremely interesting to trace this unique method of basket-weaving among all the tribes of the stock. Bands of serrate patterns are produced in color by using different wrapping threads, the principal one being grass dyed black in mud.

There is one specimen of the cedar-bark mat from Vancouver Island in which the shreded bark which serves for warp is fastened at intervals of about an inch by a chain-stitch instead of the twine. This must have been a modern innovation; at least there is not another evidence in this collection of savage acquaintance with the chain-stitch.

The Clallams, adjoining the Makahs, but of the Selish or Flathead stock, in addition to the fish-trap or bower style, are the first going southward to produce a twilled pattern over the entire surface of the vessel (Figs. 27, 28). A slight exception to this statement is the ornamentation on the brim of the Haida rain-hat. It occurs again in Mexico and among the Cherokees, Choctaws, Chetimachas, and in South America. A moment's reflection will show that the administration of the three-ply method of the Makahs is a derivation of the plicate or twisted sort. If either strand of a twist, the inner or the outer, be drawn straight, the plait will become the fish-trap pattern. In most of the Makah baskets the straight piece is laid inside the uprights, but there are examples in which it is laid outside resembling the regular plaited stitch. The Indians of this coast prior to the advent of the white man made heavy and beautiful blankets of the wool of the Rocky Mountain sheep, and of the hair of animals killed in the chase, dyed in different colors. The patterns are all geometric, and are, in fact, woven mosaics, each figure being inserted separately by twisting two woof threads backward and forward around the warp strands. Scarcely ever does the twine extend in stripes all the way across the blanket in a direct line.

Like the Haidas the Makahs prepare a great many forms of basketry for trade. A great variety of colors is used in the decoration. The hatch surface, produced by the use of three strands in weaving, gives to the basketry of this type a very unique and pleasing effect. Fig. 25 represents a common specimen of Makah basketry.

Fig. 29 shows a bottle covered with ornamental basketry. In the bottom the radiating warp is inclosed in the twined weft. The warp threads are carried over the surface of the bottle, crossing each other and producing rhomboids, after the manner of the Japanese basketry. The twined coil (Fig. 31) connects the crossings of the warp threads. This is a very interesting specimen, inasmuch as the bower or fish-trap style is replaced by the regular twined weaving of the Indians farther north.

Figs. 32, 33 represent a specimen from the Clallams, which seems to be an example of commerce. The coil is sewed on conveniently, and the ornamentation upon the sides is produced by laying the straw or quill of different color upon the regular stitching, and sewing it on one stitch over two original stitches. This is a very beautiful and strongly made specimen.

OREGON AND CALIFORNIA TRIBES.

Along the western coast of the United States from Puget Sound to Lower California are many separate stocks of Indians, quite easily recognized by the material and ornamentation of their basketry, but following two fundamental structures—the twined and the whipped coil. Some of these tribes are called Diggers because they subsist on roots, seeds, etc. It would be more reasonable to call them "basket Indians." The Klamath and the McLeod Indians of Northern California use the twined method, making water-tight and flexible baskets of great beauty (Fig. 34). The ornamentation is produced by the alternation of black and white threads in stripes and geometric figures of endless variety (Fig. 35). A very pretty coarse wallet is produced by using vertical rushes for the foundations and twining bands of two or three rows at intervals of a few inches.

The coiled and whipped structure is employed by many tribes throughout California (Figs. 36, 37, from Eel River tribe). In most of them the double coil is used; that is, two rods or osiers are carried around, or an osier overlaid with a strip of bark or yucca (See Tinné Indian baskets, page 294.) The sewing is over both and down under only the upper one of the coil just beneath. Some of the baskets of this area are of the greatest beauty, both in form, texture, and in ornamentation.

The principal shapes are the inverted truncated cone, the ginger jar, and the shallow dish or tray. From willow twigs and pine roots they weave large, round mats for holding acorn flour; various sized, flattish, squash-shaped baskets, water tight; deep conical ones of about a bushel capacity to be carried on their backs; skull caps, which are also drinking cups, worn by the squaws. They ornament the baskets by weaving in black rootlets or bark in squares, diamonds, and zigzags. (Powers: Cont. N. A. Ethnology, III, p. 47.)

On Tule River long stalks of Sporobolus are used for warps. For thread pine root is used for white, willow bark for the brown, and some unknown bark for the black. The needle is a sharpened thigh-bone of a hawk. (Id., p. 377.)

The Modok women formerly made a baby-basket of willow-work, in shape resembling a tailor's slipper or an old-fashioned watch-holder, and having various devices to shade the face. The warp is of straight rods, the woof consists of bands of twined work, just enough to hold the warp together, most of the space being left open. Some of the Northern California tribes make a baby-basket similar in shape to the Sioux and Cheyenne beaded cradle-boards.

The Californian Indians from Tulé Lake to the Gulf of California use the greatest care in securing uniformity and fineness to the foundation and the stitch. Their skill will compare favorably with that of the Siamese, who do very similar work. The needle is the long bone of a bird or mammal, the joint remaining for a handle and the point being forward of the central hard portion of the bone. The female basket-weaver pierces a hole in the fabric at the proper point, draws the thread of grass or woody fibre through the aperture, biting the end to sharpen her thread if necessary, and presses the stitches home with the bone needle.

The ornamentation is in color, pattern, and accessories. The natural color of the material is the basis of the basket. A very dark brown and a very light brown colored straw is worked into chevrons and zigzag lines in endless variety. A strip of reed or grass is sometimes carried around on the outside, concealed by two, three, or more stitches, then overlapping the same number, forming a checkered band. Beads are also laid on, and bits of worsted, even, making animal forms. The most beautiful ornament is that produced by feathers, one being laid on for each stitch, forming an imbricated covering, concealing the entire surface. When parti-colored feathers are used the effect is very wonderful.

SAHAPTIN STOCK.

In the mountains of Idaho live the Nez Percés Indians belonging to the Sahaptin stock. The Museum possesses a few samples of their basketry. Figs. 38, 39, represents a flexible wallet made of the bast of Indian hemp (*Apocynum cannabinum*). There is nothing remarkable in the manufacture of this specimen. The weaving belongs to the twined type.

The body color is the natural hue of the material. Nearly the whole surface, however, is covered with ornamentation in patterns of brown, green, red, and black. This ornamental portion is produced by the sewing of embroidery over the entire surface of the bag, the stitches passing only half way through, so that the fabric is plain on one side and ornamented on the other.

THE GREAT INTERIOR BASIN.

Leaving now the west coast, we may examine the basketry of the Great Interior Basin, including that of the Shoshones, the Apaches, the Pueblos, and the tribes living around the mouth of the Colorado.

Shoshones.—This great stock of Indians employ both structures, the twined and the whipped coil. The plaited stitch is used in the conoidal basket hats or mush bowls (Figs. 40, 41), the roasting trays (Fig. 42), and the fanning or seed gathering trays (Fig. 43), and wands (Fig. 44). The coiled and whipped structure is used in the pitched water bottles (Fig. 45), and the basket trays (Fig. 47).

Conoidal basket hats are made of willow splints or Rhus, the warp radiating from the apex, the woof splints being carried around and twined in pairs, in the manner so frequently described (Fig. 40). The woof is so thoroughly driven home as to give the appearance of the simple osier of the east. Ornamentation is produced by using one or more rows of black splints, dyed with the *Sueda diffusa*.

The roasting trays are shaped like a scoop, rimmed with a large twig (Fig. 42). The warp is made of parallel twigs laid close together, and held in place by cross plaitings about half an inch apart. It is said that Shoshones place the seeds of wild plants in these trays with hot stones and thus roast them. The specimen figured is much charred on the upper side. Dr. Edward Palmer also describes their use in fanning the hulls and epidermis of the *Pinus monophylla* seed. "The Indians remove the hulls by putting a number of nuts on a metate and rolling a flat pestle backward and forward until the hulls are loosened. The mass is then put in a flat basket tray and the hulls blown off." (Am. Nat. 1878, p. 594.)

In Schoolcraft's History of Indian Tribes, pt. 5, pls. 26, 27, will be seen Indian women gathering seeds in conical baskets, beating the plants with a spoon-shaped wand towards the basket, held in the left hand, with the mouth of the basket just under the plants (Figs. 43, 44). The baskets are made in every respect like the conoidal hats and the fans are made of twigs closely woven on the same pattern.

The water bottles belong to the coiled and whipped structure. As before mentioned, this style can be made coarse or fine, according to the material and size of the coil and the outer thread. If two twigs of uniform thickness are carried around, the stitch will be hatchy and open; but if one of the twigs is larger than the other, or if yucca or other fiber replace one of them and narrower sewing material be used, the texture will be much finer. These bottles differ in shape; one class has round bottoms, another long, pointed bottoms; one has wide mouths, another small mouths; one class has a little osier handle on the side of the mouth like a pitcher, but the majority have one or two loops of wood, horse-hair, or osier fastened on one side for a carrying strap. All of these are quite heavy, having been dipped in pitch. The same form is found among the Apaches, Mohaves, Mokis, and Rio Grande Pueblos; but it is not improbable that they were obtained from the Utes in barter or by purchase.

The basket trays of the Utes do not differ essentially in general style from those of the Gila River tribes, but they are much coarser. Among the coiled basket trays in the collection accredited to the Utes are indeed two styles, but one of them resembles so much those of their Apache neighbors on the south as to raise the suspicion that they were obtained by barter. However that may be, we are permitted to call them the Ute pattern and the Apache pattern. The Ute basket tray is made like the Ute water-bottle. A bundle of grass stems, two, three, or four, are coiled around and sewed to the upper twig of the coil just below. By the way in which the coil turns it is easy to tell whether the upper or the under surface was towards the sewer, the work always necessarily moving to the left hand. As a matter of fact, most of these coarse baskets were built up with the concave towards the workman, that side presenting a more finished appearance. On the other hand, the finer baskets, here called Apache, are coiled the other way. The foundation is a slender bundle of yucca fiber or a twig and yucca leaf combination, which enables the workman to produce a compact water-tight stitch similar to that in the California baskets just described. The Apaches understand thoroughly the use of this stitch, and their ornamental patterns in black have the greatest variety. The ornament of one specimen in the collection, supposed to be Apache, but possibly made by some California tribes, consists of a series of spiral bands widening from the bottom towards the rim; in each of the spiral bands a row of five men extends from midway in the basket to the upper edge, their places below being taken by smaller patterns* (Figs. 49–65).

Moki baskets.—Of the seven Moki pueblos six speak the Ute language. It will not be surprising also to see them making similar baskets. This is partly true and partly false. The Moki have both coiled and plaited or twined baskets. Their twined baskets are few in number. Their coiled baskets, except the water-bottles, are of a perfectly unique pattern. In addition, they use one method of work common enough in other parts of the world, but thus far unknown west of the Rocky Mountains. I speak of the common single-coiled osier or splint employed by all eastern Indians and by the negro and white basket-maker. The Moki also imitate the checker weaving of the Bella Bellas, and the twilled weaving of the Clallams.

The plaited ware of the Mokis are a few peach-baskets, made in the same manner as the Ute hats, but there is enough dissimilarity of form to give the Moki the credit of inventing this peculiar style (Figs. 66–79).

The coiled and sewed ware, aside from the water-bottles and a few bread-trays, which are evidences rather of barter than manufacture, demand our special attention. Among the Mokis and nowhere else, so far as the Museum is concerned, except in Nubia, are to be found thick-coiled baskets called sacred meal-trays, having about the concavity of old fashioned pie-plates, and varying in diameter from a few inches to over twenty. A bundle of grass or the nerves of the yucca leaf, from half an inch to an inch in diameter, is coiled around and sewed with strips of yucca leaf of uniform width, rarely exceeding the twelfth of an inch. The thread is passed regularly around the coil, drawn tightly, and passed between threads and through a few fibers of the grass in the coil beneath. It is difficult to tell whether any pains is taken to lock the threads of the coils or not. At first the coil is very small and widens as the dish enlarges. These plates are all made to be looked at inside, the coiling being invariably towards the left on the upper surface. I have not seen one exception. True to this instinct, when a Moki constructs a hat of the same material to please some white man, he makes the convex of the hat correspond to the concave of his tray, the outside of the hat being thus rough and the inside smooth. The ornamentation of these trays is produced as follows: One side of

[*NOTE.—Says Dr. E. Palmer: "In Utah, Arizona, Southern California, and New Mexico the Indians depend solely on the *Rhus aromatica*, var. *tribola* (squawberry) for material out of which to make their baskets. It is far more durable and tougher than the willow, which is not used by these Indians. The twigs are soaked in water to soften them and to loosen the bark, which is scraped off by the females. The twigs are then split by the use of the mouth and hands. Their baskets are built up by a succession of small rolls of grass, over which these twigs are firmly and closely bound. A bone awl is used to make the holes under the rim of the grass for the split twigs. Baskets made thus are very durable, will hold water, and are often used to cook in, hot stones being dropped in until the food is done." (Am. Nat. 1875, p. 598).]

the stripped yucca leaf is dark green, the other light green and white striped fading into yellow. Now by deftly turning the thread where it passes through the coil in sewing a variety of shades is produced, as in shaded worsted work. Again, by dyeing the threads black, blue, red, yellow, and combining color effects with the natural shades of the leaf, the most beautiful ornamentation is produced. There is some method in the patterns which usually commences from a blank center of a few coils with four brown spots of six stitches each. From these fundamental points all sorts of geometric figures are produced by the simple process of sewing with different-colored threads.

The coiled and decorated ozier bread-trays of the Mokis are made, I have been informed, at only one pueblo, Oraibi. The frame consists of two cross sets of twigs, from 12 to 16 in each bar of the cross. These are firmly held together at their intersection by sewing and plaiting. They then are spread out radially, the space being from time to time supplemented by additional twigs. The workman provides himself with bunches of white, yellow, orange, purple, black, blue, and green twigs only a few inches in length. These he proceeds to weave into patterns of the greatest beauty, even imitating cloud effects seen on Japanese screens, using short or long twigs as the occasion demands, hiding the ends between the ribs and the filling of the preceding coils. The process is the same as that employed by the Navahos in making the clouded blankets, and by the northwest coast Indians in their ancient mountain-sheep blankets. The greatest variety of ornament is produced, but, as in the coiled work, the center is always plain. Under the influence of trade, however, the ancient patterns are giving way to those demanded by the purchasers. As the patterns are really mosaics and could be picked out it will be easily seen that the figures on the back and front do not exactly conform, the corresponding square on the back being always one space to the right or left of the same in front.

The Moki common twig basket is as rough as rough can be; the same is true of the flat mats used about their dwellings. They are woven in the same manner as the market baskets which we are accustomed to see every day. The twilled effect on the flat mats is produced by overlapping two warp strands by each of the woof strands.

Yucca baskets and trays of a very coarse character are made by the Mokis, woven sometimes in plain checker, at other times in twill. Although the material is very coarse, quite pleasing effects are produced by the two sides of the leaf and by the different shades of the same side.

Zuñi basketry.—Although one may see at Zuñi all sorts of baskets, the most of them, including coiled or whipped trays, Moki coiled and twig basket trays, none of these are made there. The only basket of the Zuñis is their little, very rough twig peach basket, hardly worthy of notice except for its ugliness and simplicity (Figs. 80–82).

SOUTHERN INDIAN BASKETRY.

In the States of North Carolina, South Carolina, Georgia, Florida, Alabama, Mississippi, and Louisiana are many Indians still living, remnants of the Cherokees, Choctaws, Creeks, Chickasaws, and Seminoles, removed fifty years ago into the Indian Territory. Through the lowland portion of these States grow the interminable cane-brakes, and from the split cane all these tribes make their basketry. They all follow the twilled pattern of the common checker weaving. If there is any one tribe that excels it is the Choctaws, who even now expose for sale in the markets of Mobile, New Orleans, and other southern cities little baskets of green, yellow, red, and black cane, woven in twill, crossing with the woof two or more warp splints, and managing the stitches so as to produce diamonds and various zigzag patterns on the outside. They make a basket oval at the top and pointed below for presents, averring, as I was informed by a gentleman well acquainted with them, that this shape imitated the heart, which should always accompany every gift. The handles of their basketry are very clumsily put on, marring greatly the appearance of the otherwise attractive object (Figs. 85–95).

ALGONKIN AND IROQUOIS BASKETRY.

All along our northern frontier and in many parts of Canada the descendants of the once powerful Algonkin and Iroquois fabricate baskets from the birch, linden, and other white woods. The method of manufacture is universally the same: it is the plainest in-and-out weaving. The basketry is very far from monotonous, however, for the greatest variety is secured by difference of form, of color, of the relative size of the parts, and of ornamentation. In form these baskets run the whole gamut as among the Haida and the Maka, guided by the maker's fancy and the demands of trade. These Indians all live on the border of civilization and derive a large revenue from the sale of their wares. The colors are of native manufacture, red, yellow, blue, green, alternating with the natural color of the wood. By changing the relative size of the parts a great variety of effects is produced. To commence with the rudest, let us take a dozen or sixteen strips of paper half an inch wide, and cross them so as to have one-half perpendicular to the other, woven in checker at the center and extending to form the equal arms of a cross. Bend up these arms perpendicular with the woven checker and pass a continuous splint similar to the frame-work round and round in a continuous coil from the bottom to the top. Bend a hoop of wood so as to fit the top, bend down the upright splints over this, and sew the whole together with a whipping of splint, and you will have the type basket. Now, by varying the width of the splint used to cover the sides you secure a great difference of appearance. In the National Museum are baskets made of uniformly cut splints not over the one-sixteenth of an inch in width.

Finally the Algonkin and Iroquois as well as the Southern Indian know how to decorate in baskets with a great variety of rolls looking much like the napkins on the table of a hotel. He draws a splint under the warp stick, gives it a turn up or down, or two turns in different directions and draws his loose end tightly under the next warp stick but one. This operation he repeats, forming around his basket one or more rows of projecting ornaments.

CENTRAL AND SOUTH AMERICAN BASKETRY.

The Museum is not rich in South American baskets. Those from British Guiana are precisely like those described by E. im Thurn in his work entitled "Among the Indians of British Guiana." The specimens in hand are all of the twill pattern, wrought from a brown vegetable fiber which shows the same on both sides. This twill is used with good effect in the diagonally woven cassava strainers, which may be contracted in length by a corresponding increase of the width. When the grated cassava is packed into this strainer it is suspended and a great weight fastened to the bottom. The same device in cloth is used by country housewives in making curds. There is an entire lack of gaudy dyes in the Guiana baskets, the only colors being the natural hue of the wood and a jet-black varnish. The gorgeous plumage of the birds replace the dyes in ornamentation. Central American basketry does not differ greatly from that of South America except in the finish. Nothing can exceed in severe plainness and accuracy of execution the finer ware of Guiana.

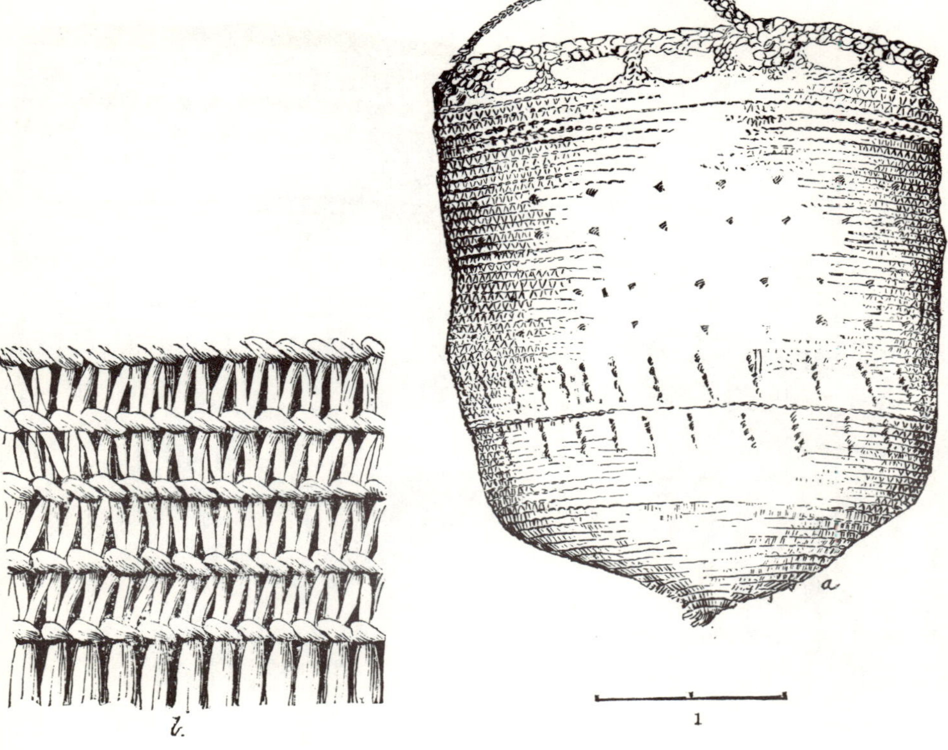

Fig. 1. Aleutian twined wallet of sea-grass. The warp consists of a number of straws radiating from the bottom. As the basket enlarges new straws are inserted, and the whole is held in place by twine made of two straws, which inclose a warp straw at each half turn. The cylindrical part of the vessel is of the diamond pattern shown in Fig. 2. The ornamentation is produced by embroidering with bits and strands of red, blue, and black worsted, in no case showing on the inside of the wallet. The continuous line between the diagonal stripes is formed by whipping with a single thread of worsted on the outer stitches of one of the twines of straw. Whipping with single thread in this ware is not common. The border is formed of the very complicated braid described in the text. Collected in Attu, by Wm. H. Dall. Museum number, 14978.

Fig. 2. A square inch of Fig. 1 enlarged, taken from the part of the texture where the rectangular meshes pass into the lozenge-shaped meshes. The peculiar method of splitting the warp threads and working the halves alternately to the right and to the left is well shown.

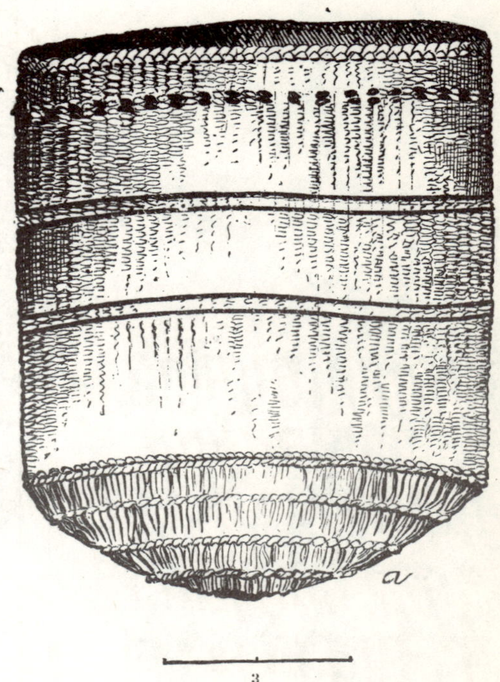

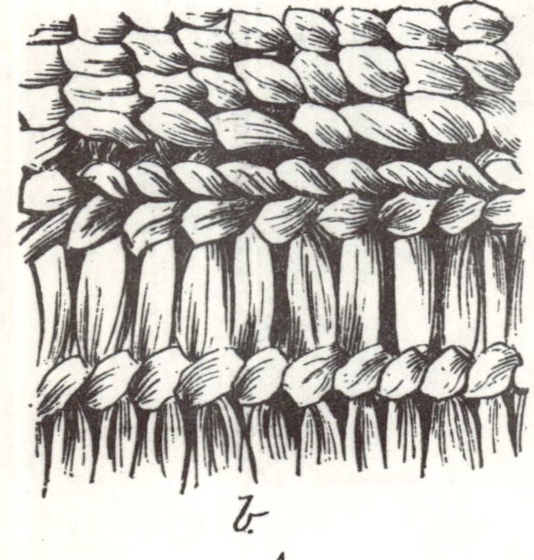

Fig. 3. Twined wallet of the Eskimo. The warp and the twining of the bottom is of a very coarse, rush-like, fiber. The bottom is in openwork and is strengthened on its outer edge by an extra twine set on externally. The body is of a dirty rush color, the spotted lines on the cylindrical portion are in black and body color. This effect may be varied by mixing two strands of different color in the twine. The fastening off at the top is done by working the warp strands into a three-ply braid, turning down on the inside of the vessel and cutting off an end whenever a new warp thread is taken up by the braid. Frequently the last three or four warp straws are not cut off but braided out to their extremities in order to form a handle. Collected at Norton Sound, by E. W. Nelson. Museum number, 38872.

Fig. 4. One square inch of Fig. 3, representing (1) four rows of twining on the cylindrical portion; (2) the method of adding a new row of twining externally for a boundary between the bottom and the cylindrical portion, and (3) the method of forming an open-work bottom.

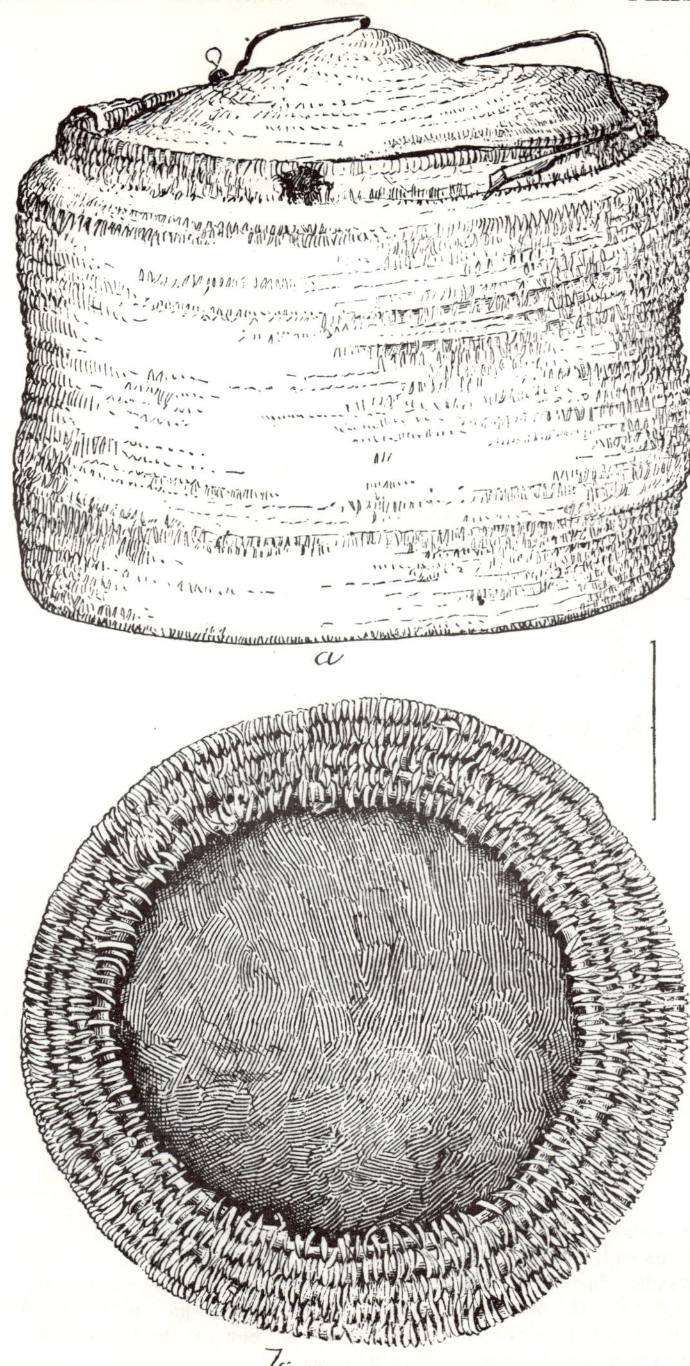

FIG. 5. Coiled Eskimo basket. The bottom is a bit of old leather, to which is sewed, by means of grass thread, a coil of straws varying in thickness from ⅛ to ¼ inch. This coil is continued to form the cylindrical side, the shoulder at the top, and the neck. The disk-like cover is made in the same manner. Collected by E. W. Nelson, in Norton Sound. Museum number, 38469.

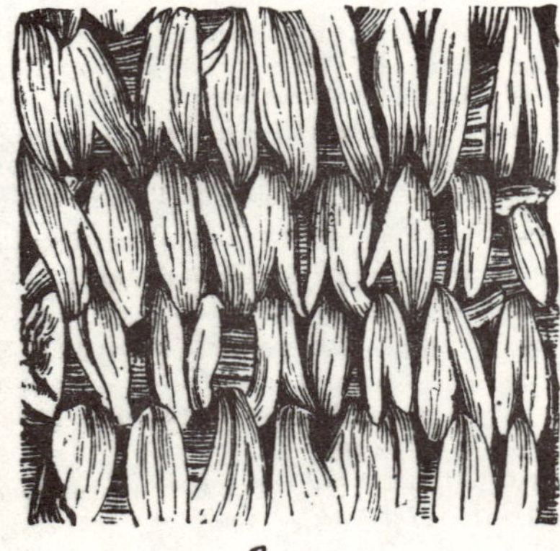

C.

Fig. 6. One square inch of Fig. 5 enlarged, showing the bunch of straws used as the body of the coil, and the manner of whipping the turns of the coil with grass threads. Instead of carefully looping the thread into the one just below, as is done in the best coiled work, the basket-maker passed the sticks indiscriminately through or between those below. Some of the Eskimo baskets, however, resemble those of the next class.

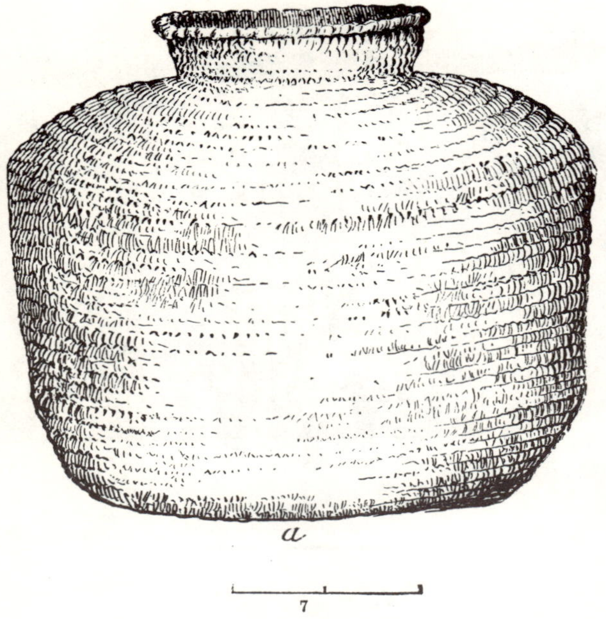

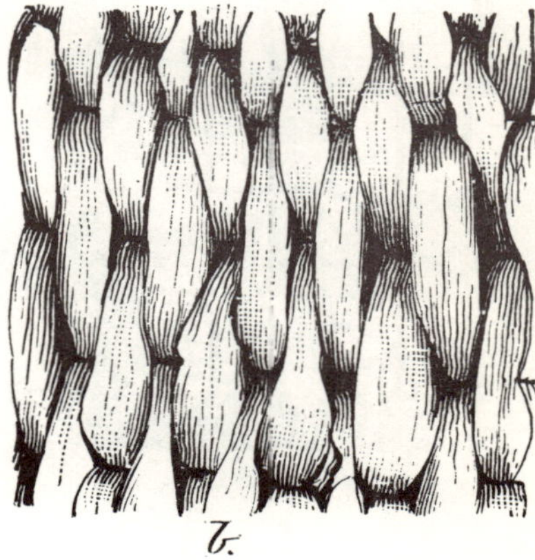

8

FIG. 7. Coiled basket of the Tinné or Athabascan Indians of Alaska and British America. The warp or foundation is a single osier or spruce root, the sewing is done with small splints of spruce root. The stitches vary from $\frac{1}{8}$ to $\frac{1}{4}$ inch in length, and the splints from $\frac{1}{16}$ to $\frac{1}{8}$ inch in width. The stitches of each coil are locked into the stitches of the coil beneath in addition to passing under the fundamental rod. In some cases the Eskimo fashion of splitting the threads in sewing appears, but the evidence shows that the Tinné were the teachers of the Eskimo, and the latter follow only the ruder work of their preceptors. The general shape of this class of baskets is that of a low narrow-mouthed jar. Collected by Lucien M. Turner, Lower Yukon River. Museum number, 24342.

FIG. 8. One square inch of Fig. 7, showing the method pursued in coiled basketry with a single fundamental and a single splint of osier or spruce root.

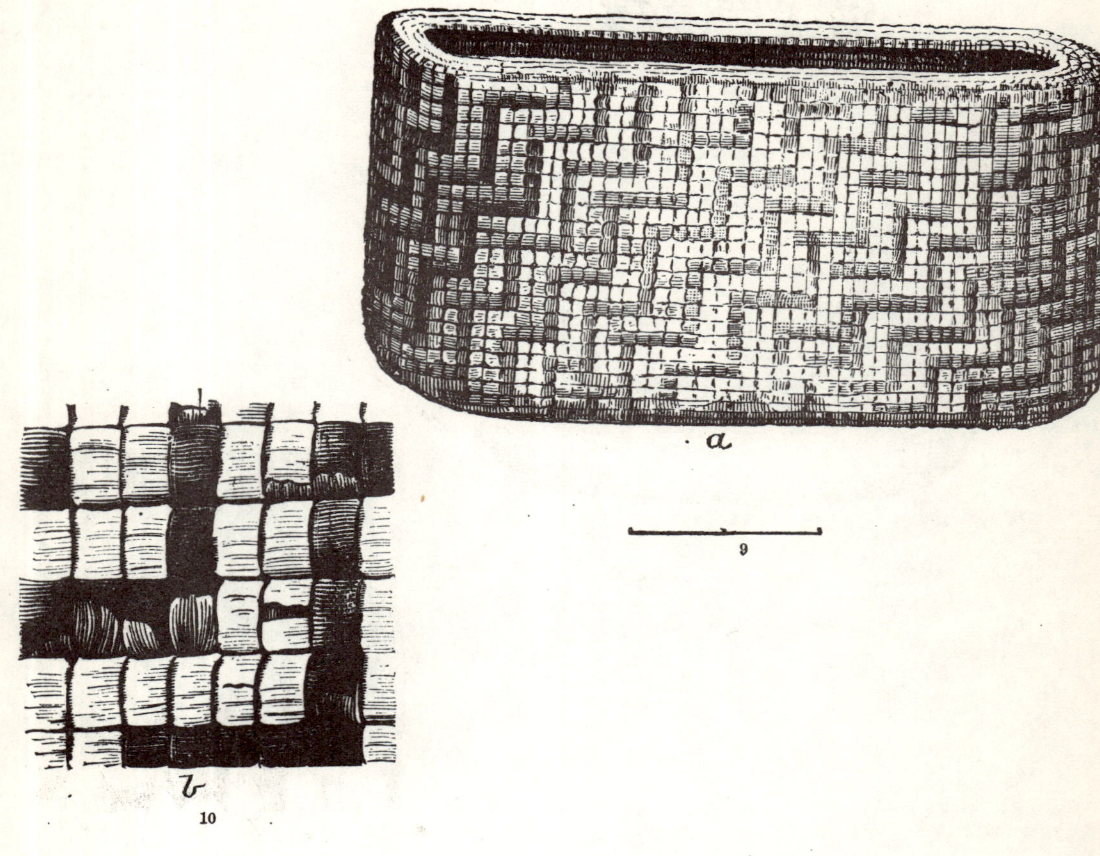

FIG. 9. Alaskan Indian coiled basket. The outer portion is so covered with ornament as to conceal the texture of the basket, which is built up by whipping a coil of rushes or small splints with splint or birch bark. The bottom of this basket is not a coil, but a number of straight foundation rods sewed into a rectangular mat, around this the sides are built up by coiling. The elaborate ornamentation is described under Fig. 10. Collected in Alaska, by J. J. Maclean, in 1882. Museum number, 60235.

FIG. 10. One square inch of Fig. 9, showing the elaborate ornamentation. The imbricated effect upon the surface is produced by sewing on little loops of bark and straw, white and brown, with blind stitches in such a way as to conceal the manner of attachment. The mat-like bottom is ornamented by sewing on straws longitudinally with stitches wide apart, so as to show a checker pattern of straw and stitching. This method of ornamenting the bottom is often pursued over the whole external surface of the basket.

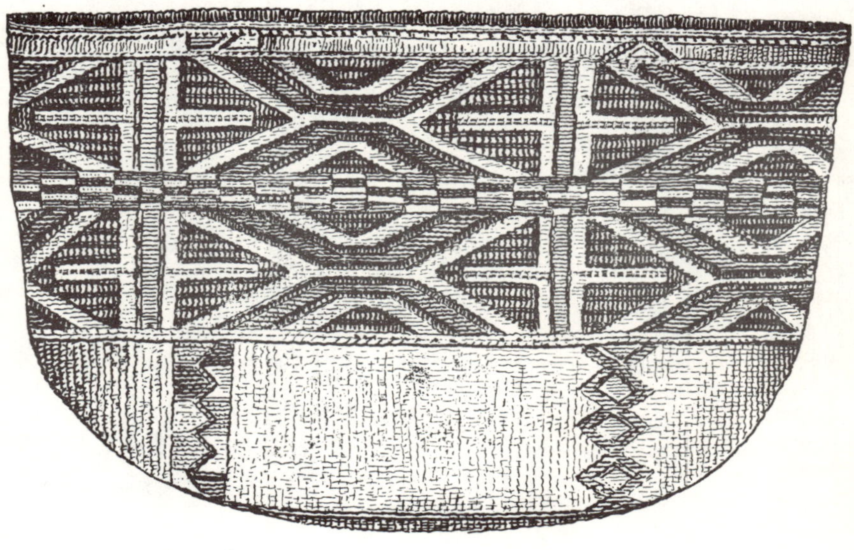

FIG. 11. Twined basket-wallet of the Chilkaht Indians (Thlinkit stock), band-box shape when spread out. The bottom is very roughly made of spruce-root splints, warp and twine, the former radiating from the center. The boundary of the bottom is a single row of twine fastened on externally. The cylindrical portion for a few inches above the bottom is in natural brown color, excepting two or three vertical bands of embroidery. The rest of the body is in stripes of natural color, black and Indian red. The border is formed by turning under the warp threads and cutting them off. The geometric patterns (different on every wallet) are formed by embroidering upon the outer surface, half through the fabric, with yellow, light red straws and spruce-root dyed. This style of basketry is followed by the Haidas in the baskets made for sale. Collected at Sitka, Alaska, by Dr. J. B. White, in 1876. Museum number, 21560.

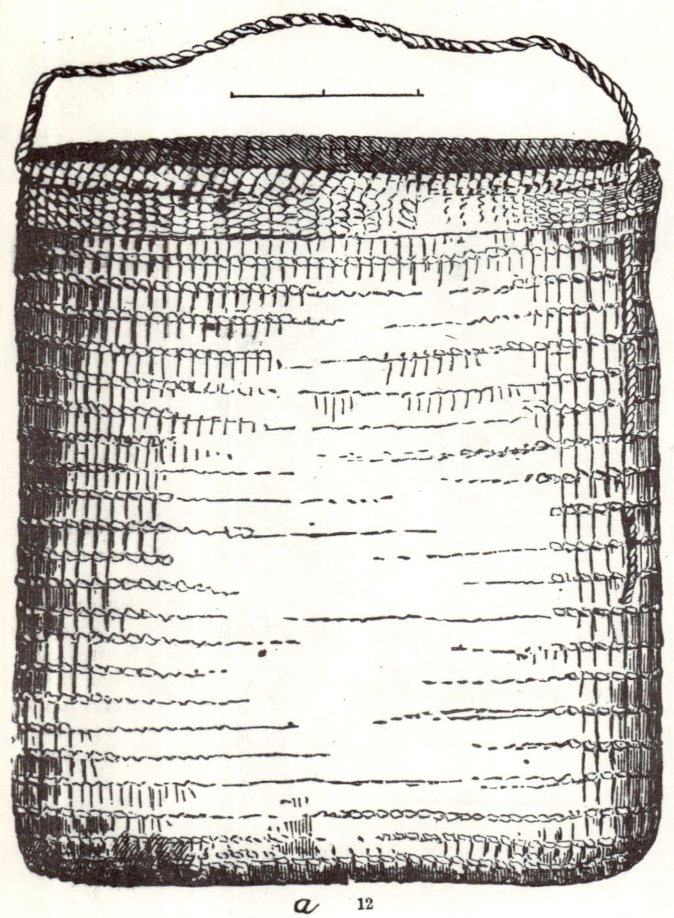

a 12

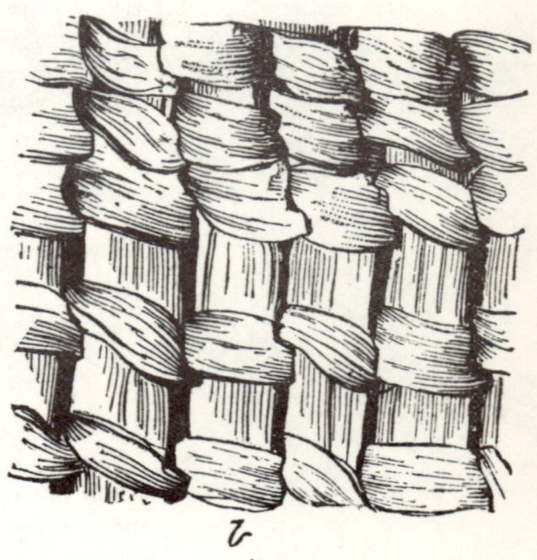

b 13

Fig. 12. Twined basket of spruce root, made by Haida Indians. This specimen snows better than any of the preceding the method of administration in the twined basketry. The handle is a twine of spruce root fastened on by weaving in and out on the side, the lower end knotted. The fastening off at the rim is done by bending down the warp threads externally and sewing them flat with one row of twining. Collected by James G. Swan, in Queen Charlotte Archipelago, in 1883. Museum number, 88964.

Fig. 13. One square inch of Fig. 12 taken near the top, so as to show the close and the open weaving. The method of twine weaving is perfectly shown in this figure.

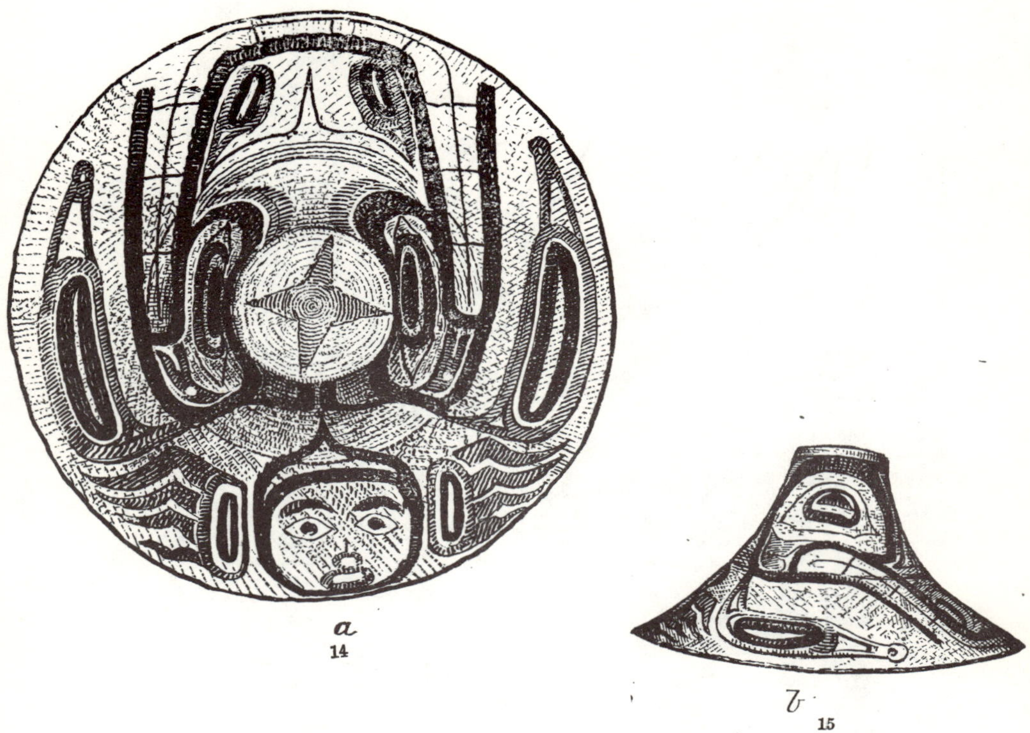

Fig. 14. Rain hat of twined basketry in spruce root from Haida Indians, reduced to one-eighth linear. This figure is the upper view and shows the method of ornamentation in red and black paint. The device in this instance is the epitomized form of a bird, the first step from pictures toward graphic signs. Omitting the red cross on the top, the beak, jaws, and nostrils are shown above; the eyes at the sides near the top, and just behind them the symbol for ears. The wings, feet, and tail, inclosing a human face, are shown on the margin. The Haida as well as other coast Indians from Cape Flattery to Mount Saint Elias cover everything of use with totemic devices in painting and carving. Collected in Queen Charlotte Archipelago, by J. G. Swan. Museum number, 89033.

Fig. 15. Showing the conical shape of Fig. 14. This form should be compared with one seen so frequently in Chinese and Japanese hats. On the inside a cylindrical band of spruce root is stitched on so as to make the hat fit the wearer's head. A string passed under the chin is frequently added.

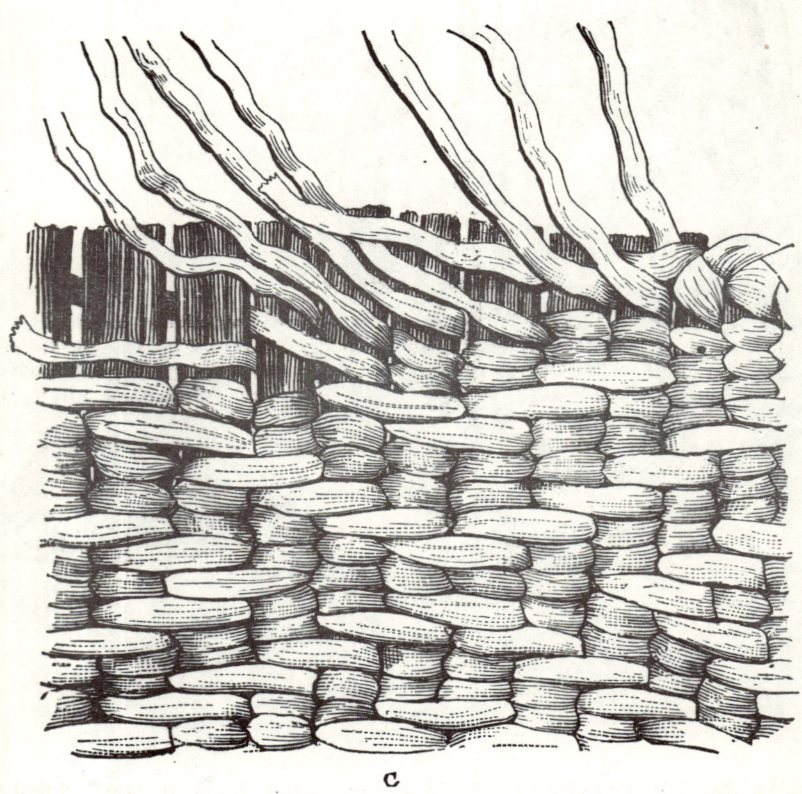

C

FIG. 16. A portion 1¼ by 1 inch, taken from the rim of the last two figures. It shows the regular method of twined weaving, the introduction of the skip-stitch or twilled weaving into the greatest variety of geometric patterns, and the ingenious method of fastening off by a four-ply braid showing only on the outer side.

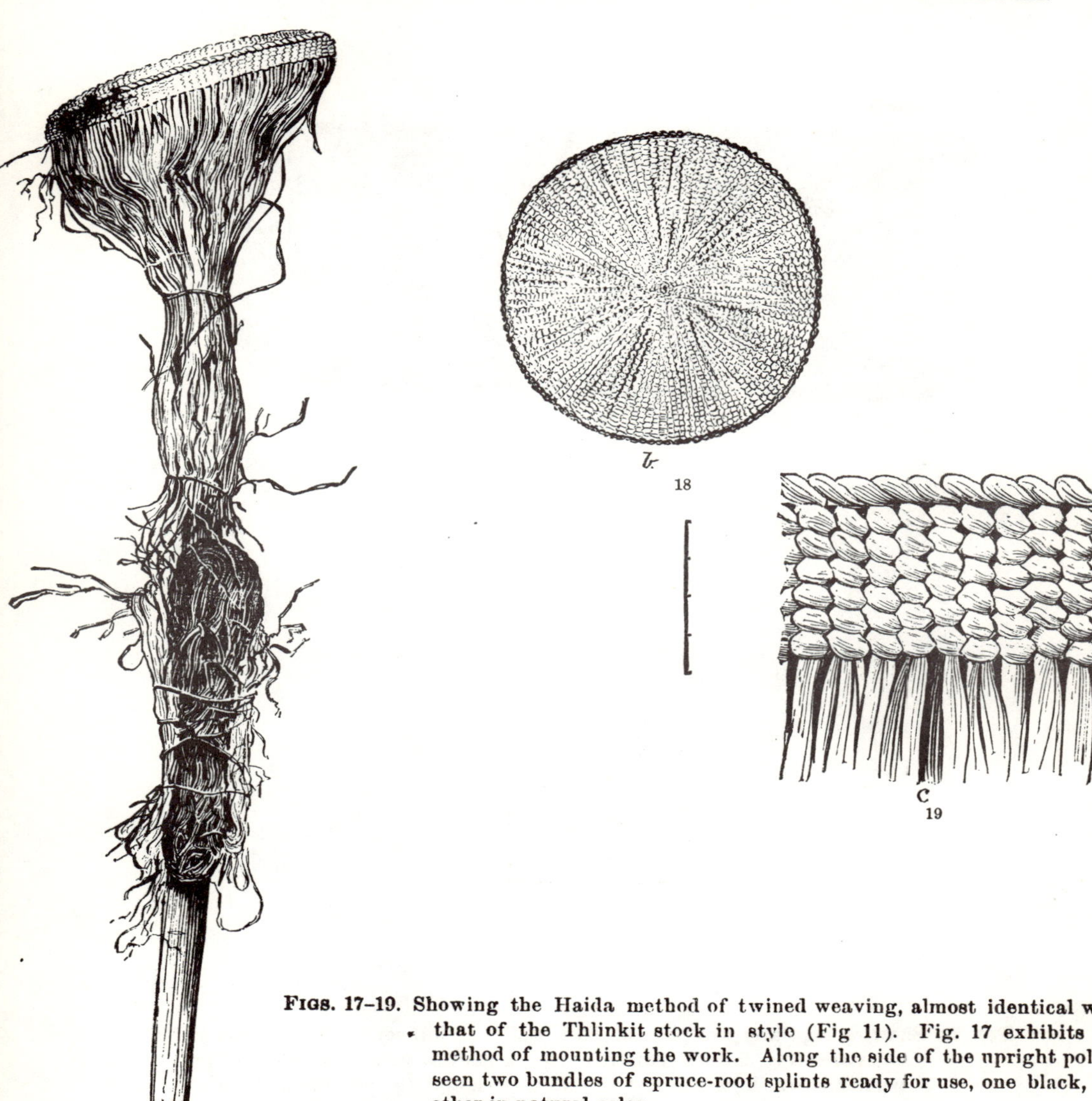

FIGS. 17–19. Showing the Haida method of twined weaving, almost identical with that of the Thlinkit stock in style (Fig 11). Fig. 17 exhibits the method of mounting the work. Along the side of the upright pole is seen two bundles of spruce-root splints ready for use, one black, the other in natural color.

FIG. 18. The bottom of the basket, with radiating warp, twined weft, and an external twine on its outer boundary.

FIG. 19. One square inch of Fig. 17, indicating the exceedingly regular method of the twining. On the upper margin is seen the external row of twining added after the fabric was finished. Collected from the Massett tribe of Haidas, Queen Charlotte Islands. Museum number, 88956.

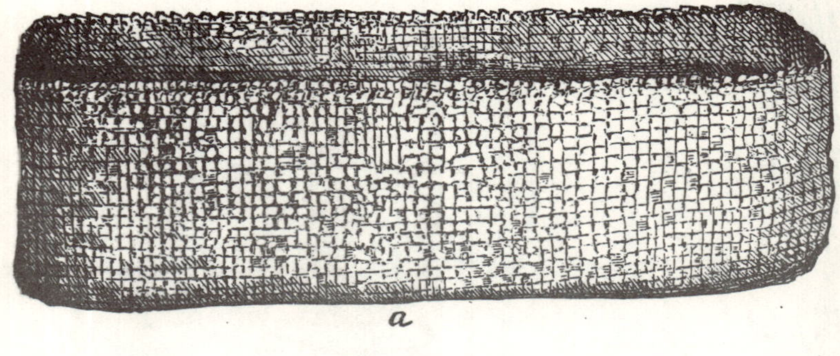

20

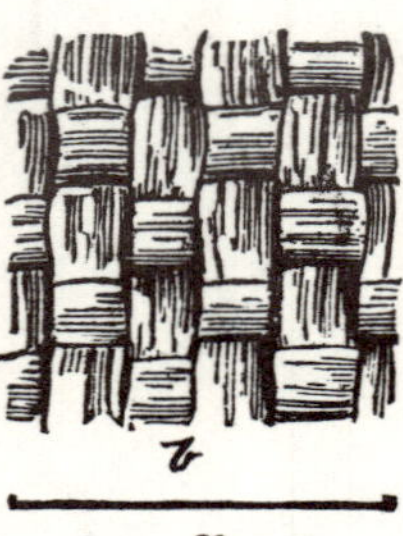

21

Fig. 20. Showing regularly woven cedar-bark wallet of Bilhoolas. The bottom and sides are all in checker pattern. By an endless variety in real and proportional width of warp and weft thread, and by coloring some of the threads, an infinite number of patterns is produced. The fastening off is done as in Fig. 12. In many cedar-bark baskets of this region the two sets of threads run diagonally, producing a diamond rather than a checker pattern. Again, much more rarely three elements are involved, an open-work of two sets running diagonally, and a horizontal thread running through the open rhombs, in and out, as in multitudes of Japanese baskets. Collected in British Columbia, by James G. Swan.

Fig. 21. One square inch of Fig. 20, natural size.

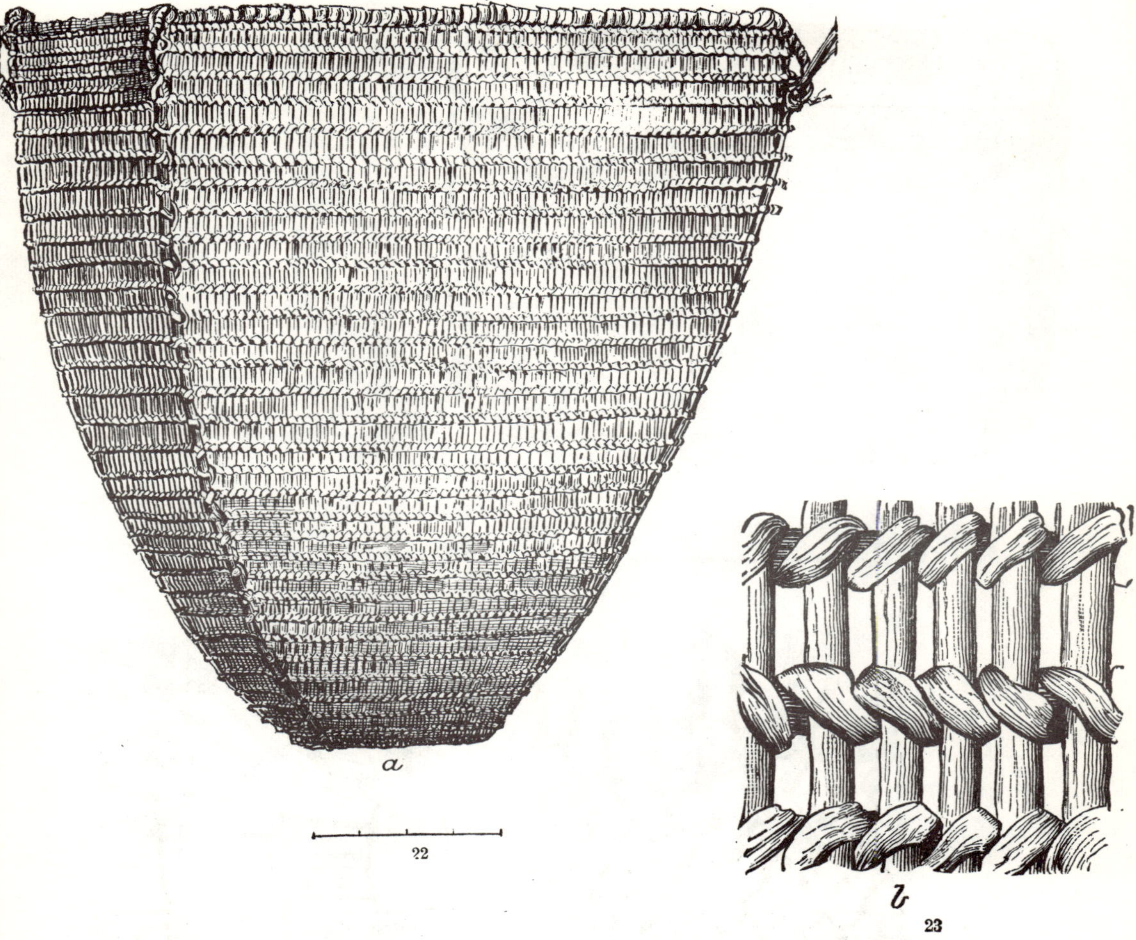

Fig. 22. Openwork carrying basket of the bird-cage or fish-trap style of weaving made by the Clallam Indians (Selish stock). The frame-work is a rectangle of large twigs from the corners of which depend four twigs, joining as shown in the figure. To this frame-work are lashed smaller rods running horizontally and vertically, making a lattice-work with any desirable size of meshes. Finally, spruce-root splints are coiled around the crossings of these lattice rods. In this particular example the coiling is not continuously around the basket, but on each side separately in boustrophedon, but in the pretty Makah baskets, woven in this style, the coiled thread continues around without break from the beginning to the end of the work. The handles for the attachment of the head-strap are loops of spruce-root cord set on at the corners. Collected in Washington Territory, by J. G. Swan. Museum number, 23480.

Fig. 23. Showing the exact method administration in this form of basketry. It should be closely studied with reference to Makah basketry and Congo shields and baskets.

PLATE XIV.

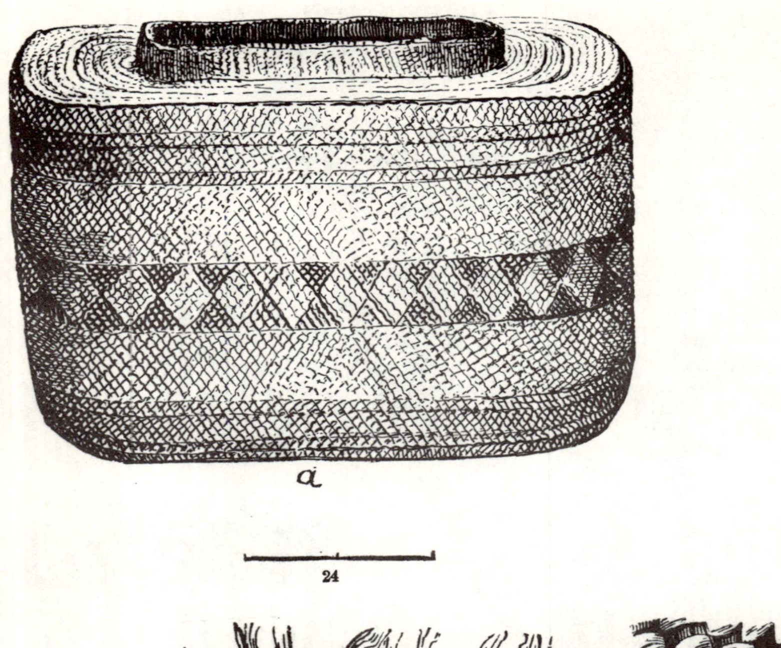

24

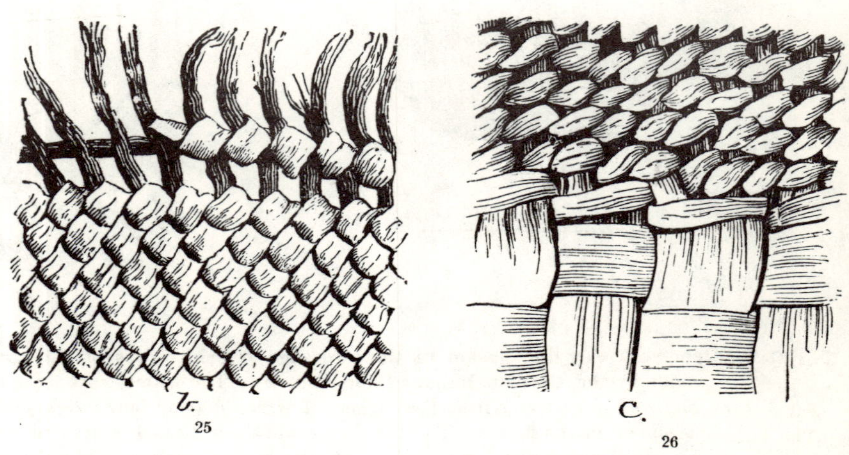

25

26

FIGS. 24–26. A wonderful specimen of basketry from the Makah Indians (Nutkan stock). It includes the three distinct types, the plain checker weaving of the Bilhoolas (Fig. 26, bottom), the twined pattern frequently mentioned in this paper, and, lastly, the bird-cage pattern of the Clallams (Fig. 25). The ornamentation on this class of baskets, as on the commercial baskets of the Haidas, consists of geometric patterns in black, yellow, drab, reds, blues, &c., colors many of which are obtained from traders. The straws are dyed and the pattern is alike on both sides. Collected at Cape Flattery, by James G. Swan, in 1876. Museum number, 23346.

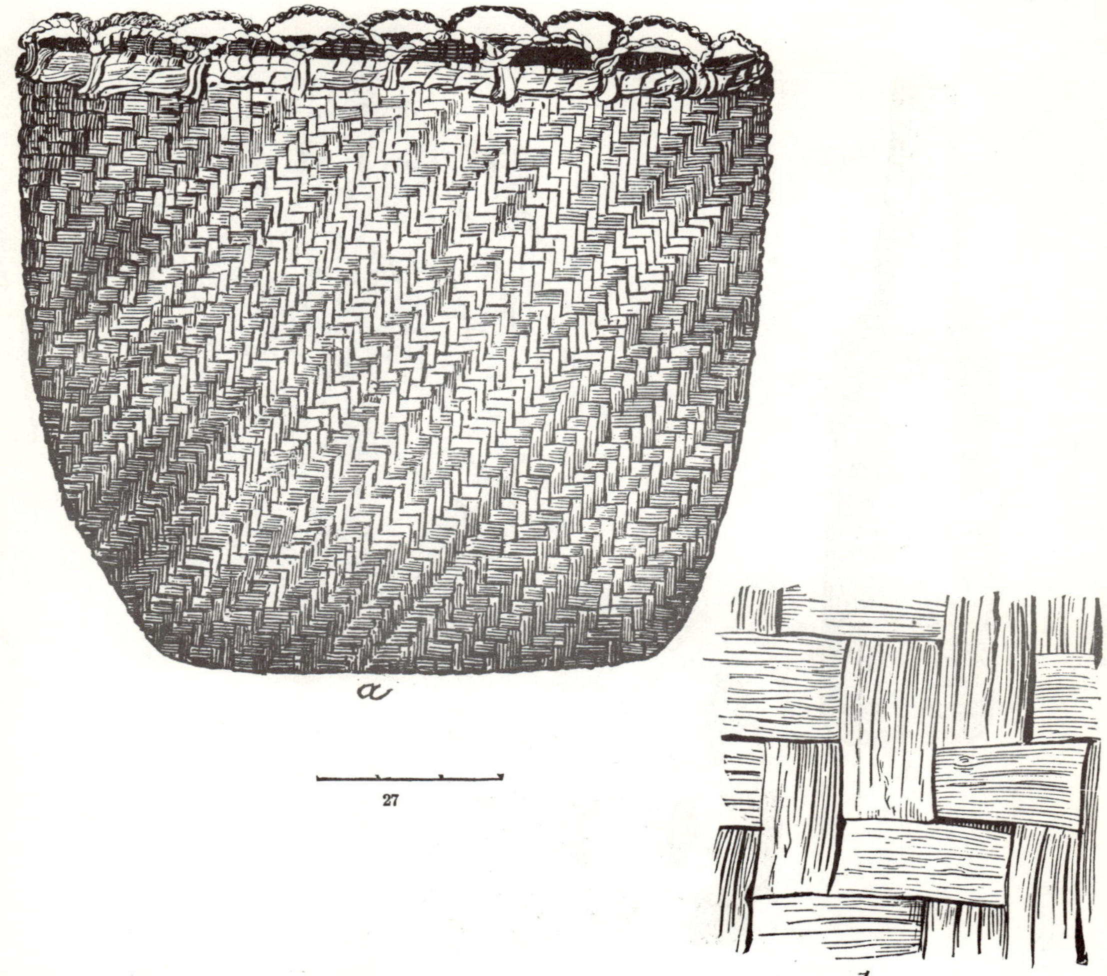

Fig. 27. Twilled splint basket of the Clallams (Selish stock), made of white birch wood. The bottom was woven first and all of the bottom splints became the warp of the sides, which are built up by weaving weft splints. The twilled effect is produced by passing each weft splint always over two warp splints, and by carrying two weft splints around at the same time, making them overlap alternate warp splints. The fastening off is done by bending down the warp straws and whipping them in place with splint. The scallop on the edge is formed by looping the middle of two splints under the rim, twisting both pairs of ends into a twine, passing one twine through the other, and then doubling down to repeat process for the next scallop. Collected in Washington Territory, by James G. Swan. Museum number, 23509.

Fig. 28. One square inch of Fig. 27, showing the method of administering the splints in plain twill. Innumerable pleasing effects are produced by varying the color, number, width, and direction of the splints overlapping in the weaving.

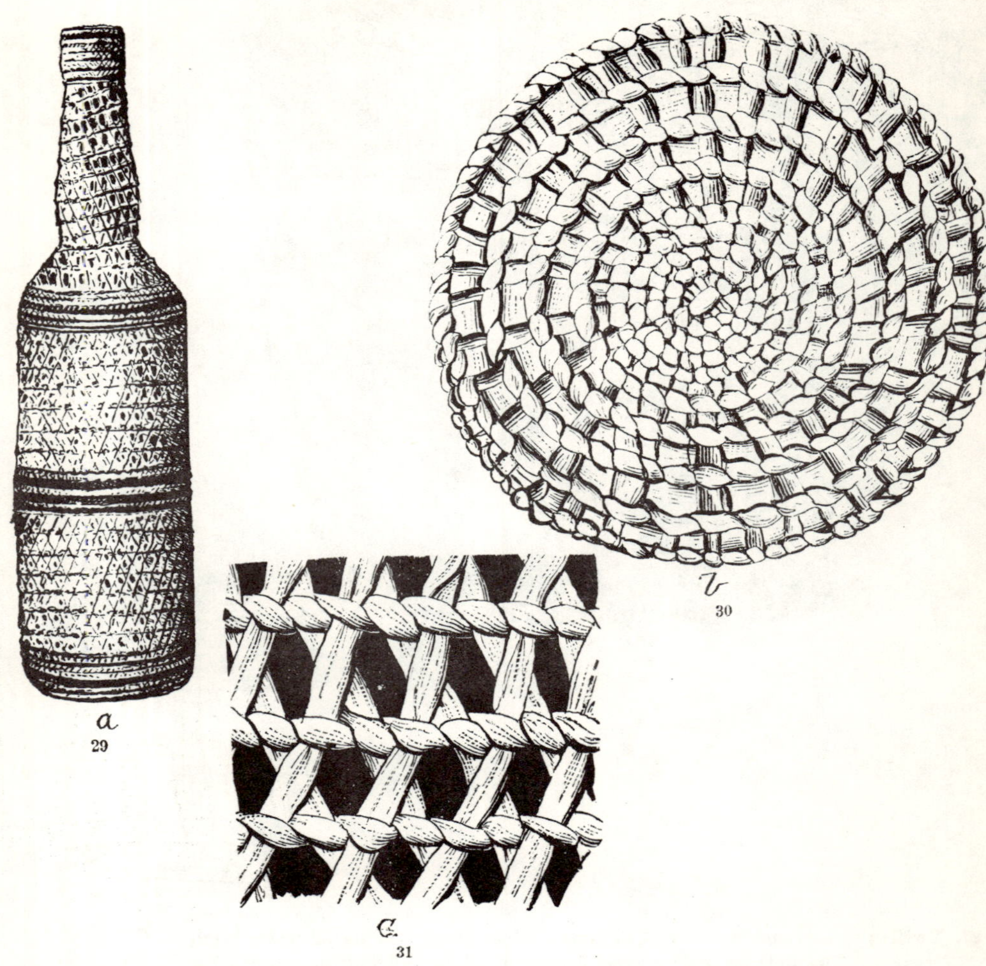

Fig. 29. Bottle covered with basket-work by Makah Indians. The groundwork is of bast and the ornamentation of red, yellow, and black straws sewed on singly after the Makah fashion. Great numbers of these covered bottles and other fanciful forms are prepared for sale by the Makahs as well as by the Haidas, whose work is similar in external appearance, but not in the method of weaving. Collected at Neeah Bay, Washington Territory, by James G. Swan, in 1884. Museum number, 73755.

Fig. 30. Bottom of Fig. 29, showing the radiated warp and the alternation of twined weft with the ordinary in-and-out weaving.

Fig. 31. Portion of the side of the bottle, showing the lattice arrangement of the warp, and the twined weft, producing irregular hexagons. This method of producing polygonal meshes, excepting the twined weft, is pursued in great variety and with excellent effect by the Japanese and other Oriental peoples.

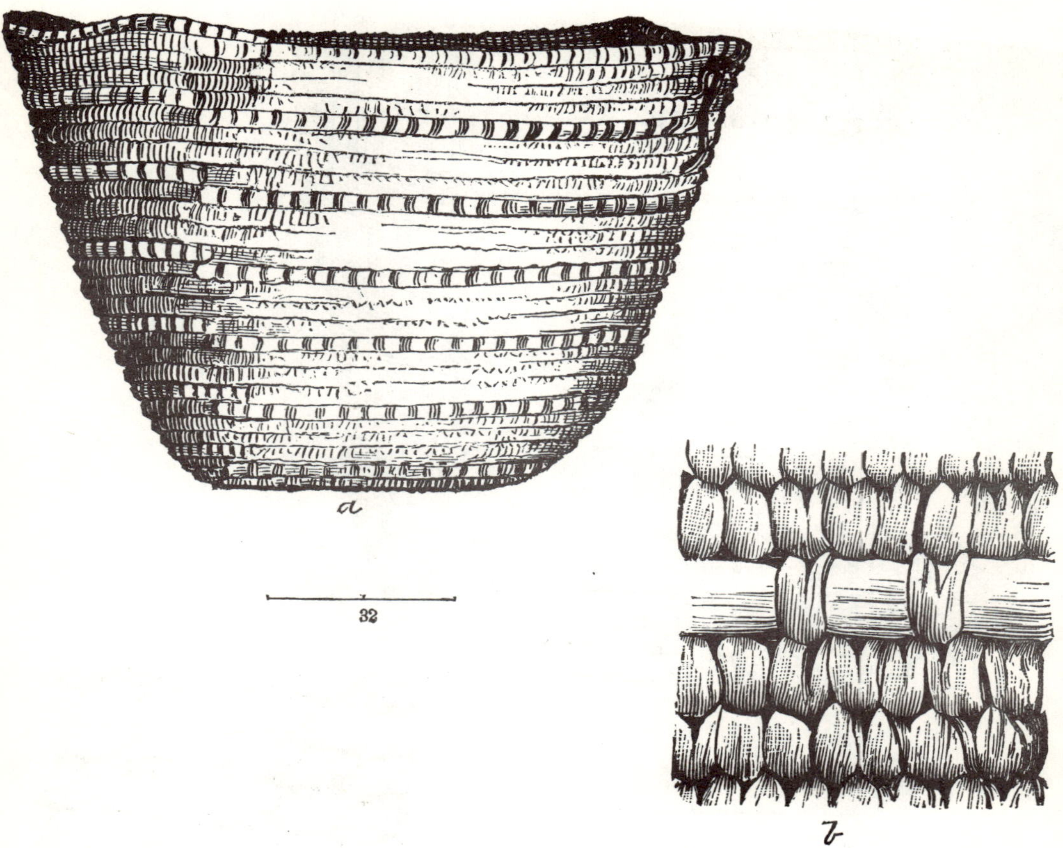

33

FIG. 32. Coiled basket, made of single osier coil, sewed down with spruce root or willow fiber, ascribed to Clallams by commerce in the text, but found on examination to have come from Sitka. The sewing is very regularly done, but the stitches split one another, as in Eskimo coiled sewing. Collected at Sitka, by J. G. Swan, in 1876. Museum number, 23512.

FIG. 33. One square inch of 32, showing the method of adding ornamental straws, caught by every third stitch. The appearance of the yellow dots on the dark-brown ground is very pleasing in the original.

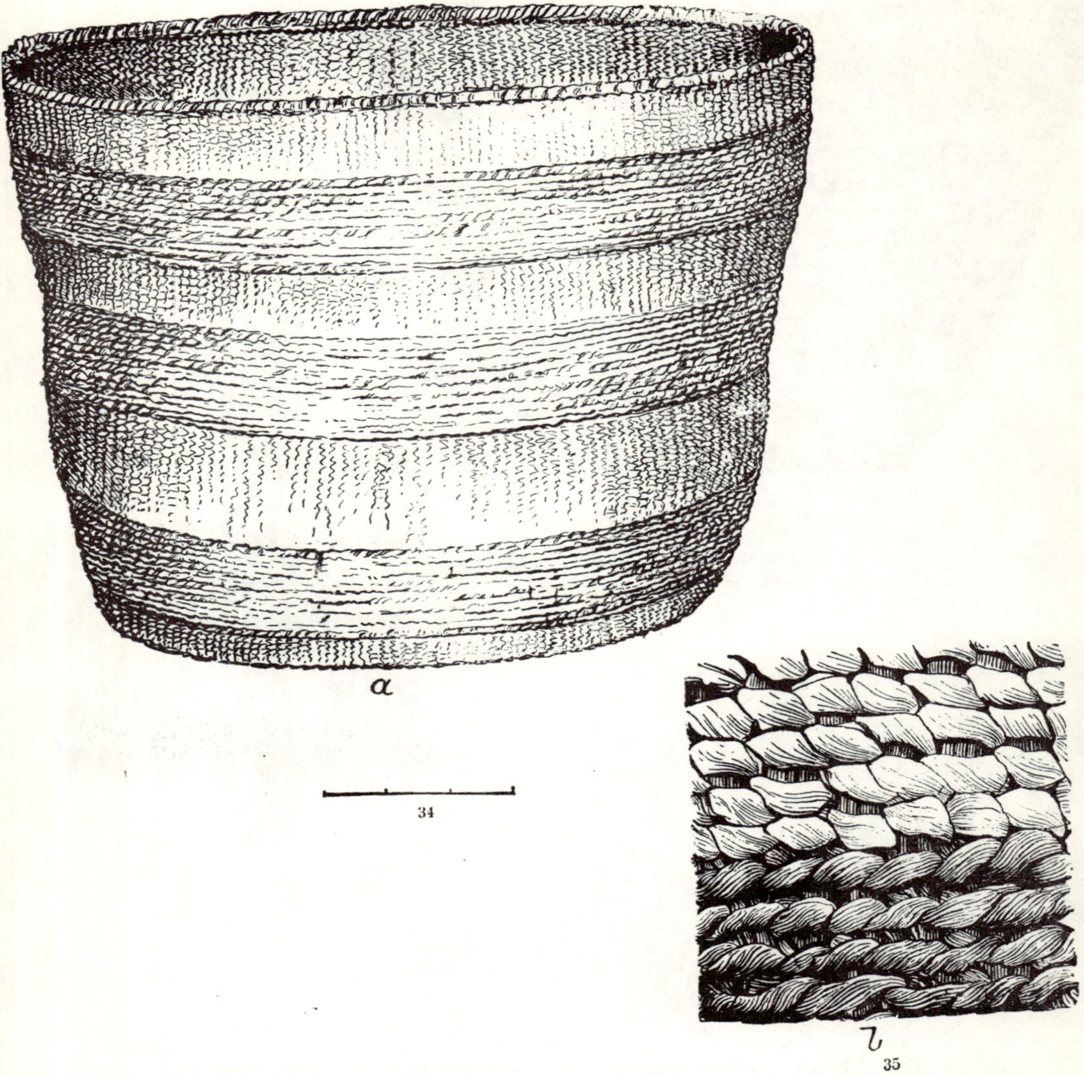

Fig. 34. Twined or plaited flexible basket of the Klamath Indians, made of rushes and straw. The management of the material is precisely as in the Eskimo wallets (Fig. 3). The three elevated bands upon the outside are formed by rows of twine set on externally. The border in this case is formed by binding down the warp straws and sewing them fast with trader's twine. By twining a dark and a light colored straw, two dark or two light straws, and by varying the number of these monochrome or dichrome twines, very pleasing effects in endless variety are produced. Collected at Klamath Agency, in 1876, by L. S. Dyar. Museum number, 24124.

Fig. 35. One square inch of 34, showing the appearance of the body weaving above and of the ornamental twining below.

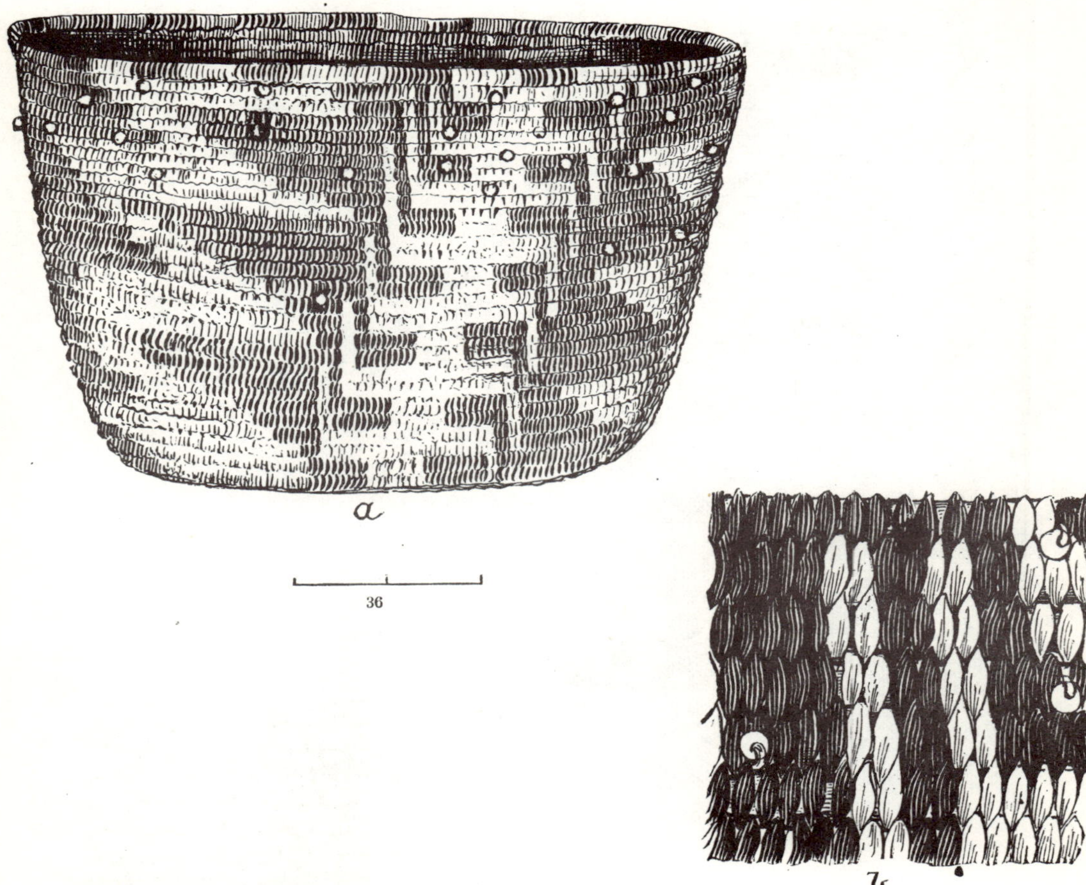

Fig. 36. Coiled and whipped baskets from Hoochnom tribe, made of some species of pliable root. The bottom is started upon a small flat Turk's-head knot of splint ⅜ of an inch in diameter, and continued in a plane outward 4 inches in diameter before any ornament is attempted. The coils are ⅛ inch in cross-section and there are twenty stitches to the inch. There are three pairs of the ornament on the exterior all alike. The harmony of geometric design produced by inverting the triangles on the alternate sides is much more expressive in the specimen where the brown-black ornament is in contrast with the dark wood color of the body. This specimen should be compared with Fig. 56. The patterns and designs in this ware are of great variety and beauty, and the use of beads and feathers much improves their appearance. Collected at Eel River, California, by Stephen Powers, in 1876. Museum number, 21371.

Fig. 37. One square inch of Fig. 36, showing method of coiling with various colored straws.

PLATE XX.

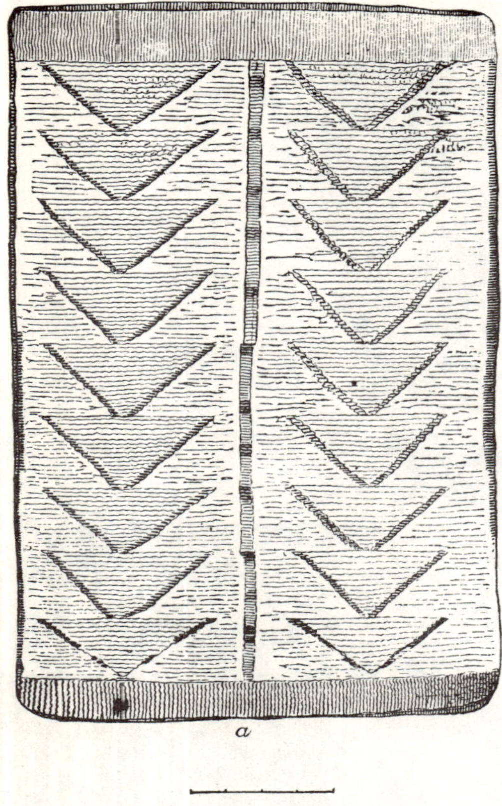

38

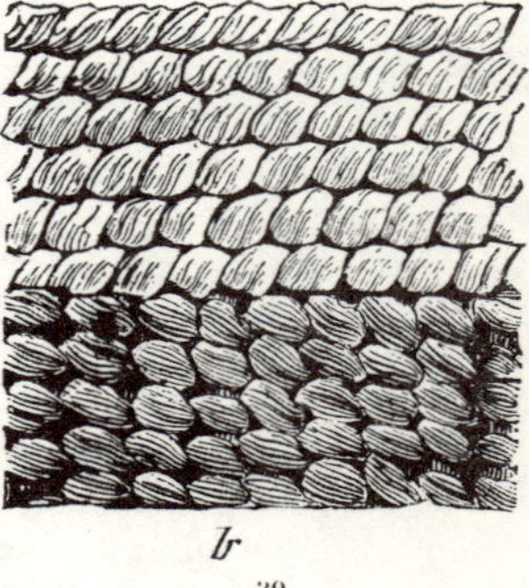

39

FIG. 38. Twined wallet of Nez Percé Indians (Sahaptin stock) made of the bast of Indian hemp (*Apocynum cannabinum*). A sufficient number of warp strands were stretched and joined together in their middle by one row of twining. The ends of these warp strands were then brought together, and the weaver, by continuing the twine around and around, built up her bag. The ornamentation is the same old story of straw colored, brown, blue, and green strings of the Indian hemp twined externally. Collected in Idaho, by Rev. George Ainslee. Museum textile number, 8025.

FIG. 39. One square inch of Fig. 38, showing the body twining and the twined ornament above.

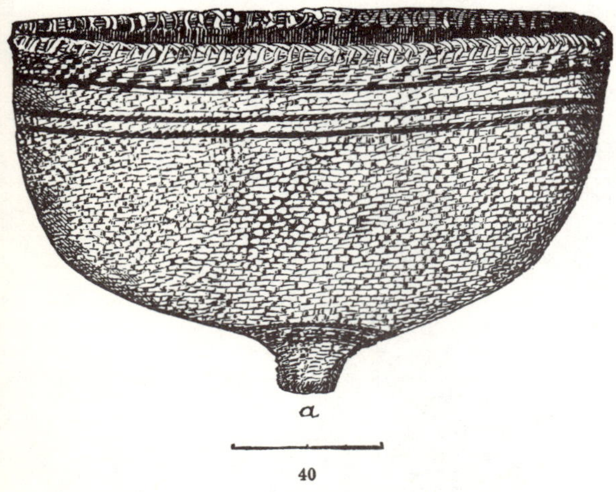

a

40

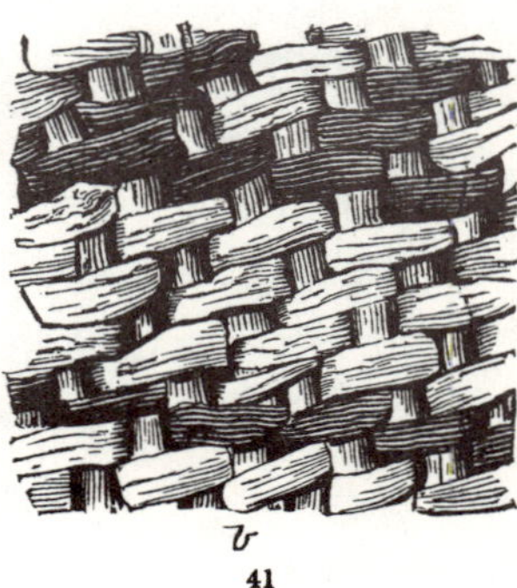

b

41

FIG. 40. Twined basket hat of the Utes, used by women either as a hat or as a basket. The California women make hats of a similar pattern, but much finer. The warp twigs converge at the bottom and additional ones are added as the texture widens. The weft splints are carried around in pairs and twined so as to inclose a pair of vertical twigs, producing a twilled effect something like that of the softer ware of the Haidas and Clallams. The border of this twined basket is very ingeniously made. First, the projecting warp sticks were bent down and whipped with splints to form the body of the rim. Then with two splints the weaver sewed along the upper margin, catching these splints alternately into the warp straws below, giving the work the appearance of a button-hole stitch. The ornamentation is produced by means of dyed twigs either alone or combined with those of natural color. The texture of this ware is always coarse and rigid owing to the lack of good material in this arid region. Collected in Southern Utah, by J. W. Powell. Museum number, 11838.

FIG. 41. One square inch of Fig. 40, showing method of weaving and administering the colored splints.

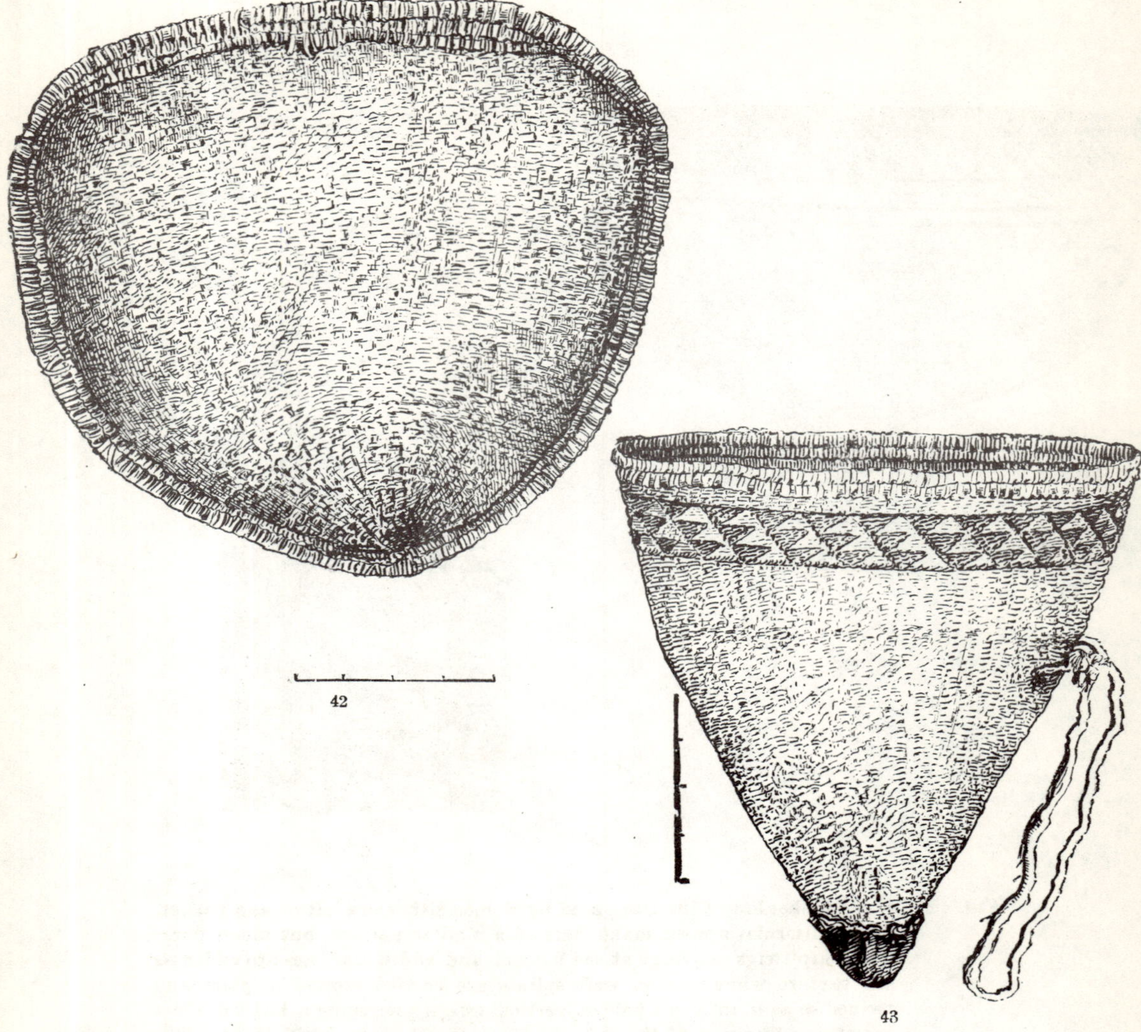

FIG. 42. Twined roasting-tray of the Pai Utes. The warp is a lot of osiers spread out like a fan. The weaving commenced at the bottom by short curves and progressed by ever-widening curves to the outer margin. The rim is made by a double row of the coiled and whipped work. The whole surface is very rough, as in all Ute work, by reason of not twisting the strands when making the twine. There is little ornamentation on this class of objects. Collected in Southern Utah, in 1874, by Maj. J. W. Powell. Museum number, 11857.

FIG. 43. Twined gathering and carrying basket of the Pai Utes. Woven precisely as the hats (Fig. 40) and the roasting-trays (Fig. 42). The splints are very fine, but their refractory nature makes all this ware coarse. Ornamentation is produced by external twining and by geometric patterns in dyed splints. Collected in Southern Utah, by J. W. Powell, in 1874. Museum number, 14667.

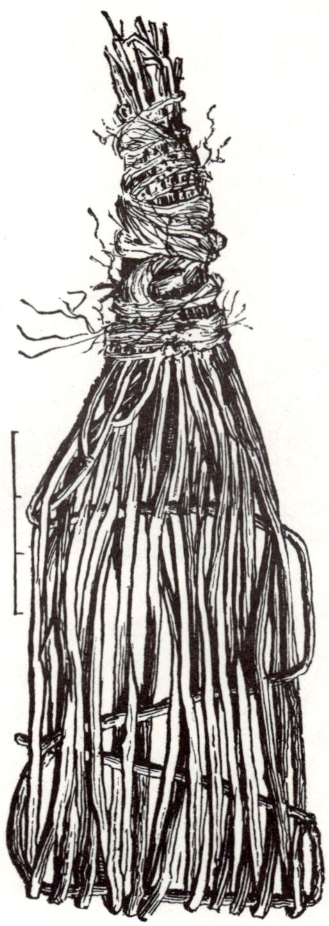

Fig. 44. Harvesting wand of Pai Utes, made of twigs, split or whole, bound with yucca fiber. The figure represents the coarsest specimen in the collection. In most of this class the longitudinal twigs are held in place by rows of twine at long intervals. Collected in Southern Utah, in 1874, by J. W. Powell. Museum number, 11823.

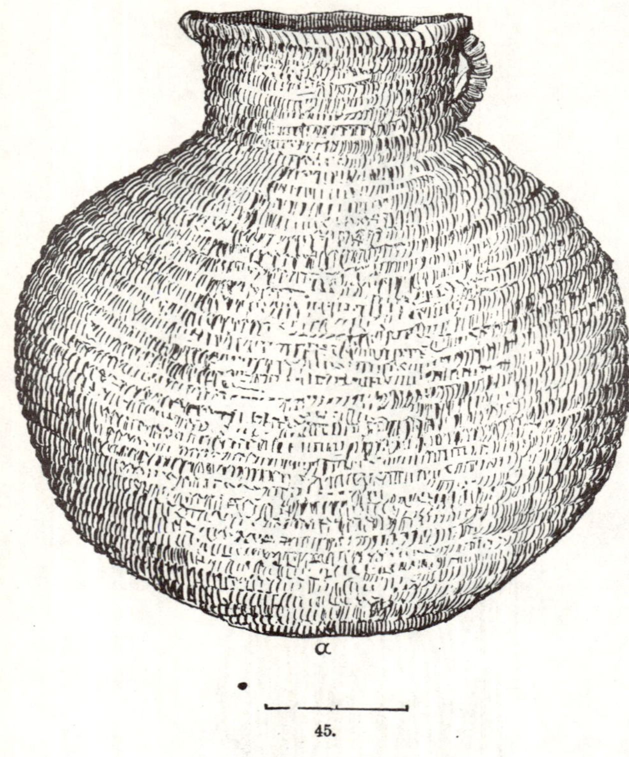

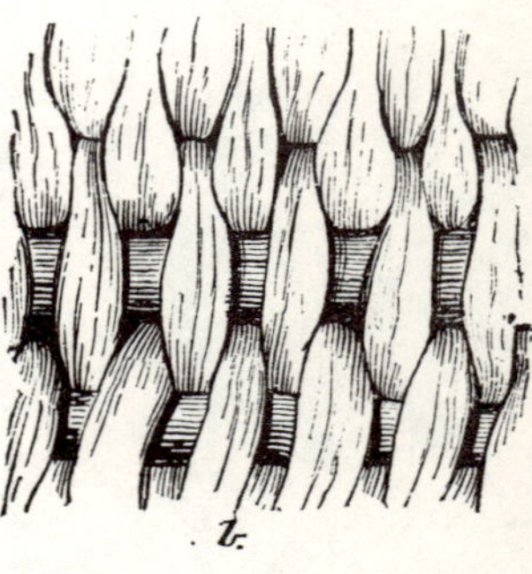

FIG. 45. Coiled and pitched bottle of the Pai Utes, made of osier, by coiling the fundamental twigs in pairs and sewing with split osier always over the two in hand and between the twigs of the preceding round. As this bottle is to be covered with pitch either inside or out or on both sides, the sewing is left very open. By having one twig large and the other very small or by having a bunch of grass for the two twigs, a water tight joint is produced by the swelling of the warp and weft. The bungling manner of administering the stitches reminds one of the same type of ware among the Eskimo. A great variety of form is given to these pitched bottles. Collected in Southern Utah, by J. W. Powell, in 1874. Museum number, 11262.

FIG. 46. One square inch of Fig. 46, showing the use of the double-twig coil.

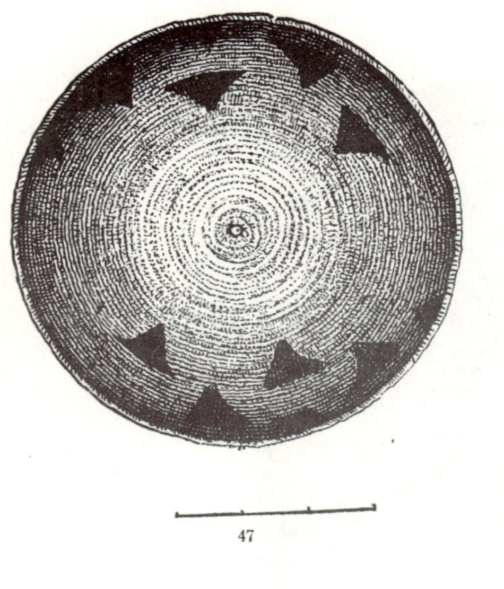

47

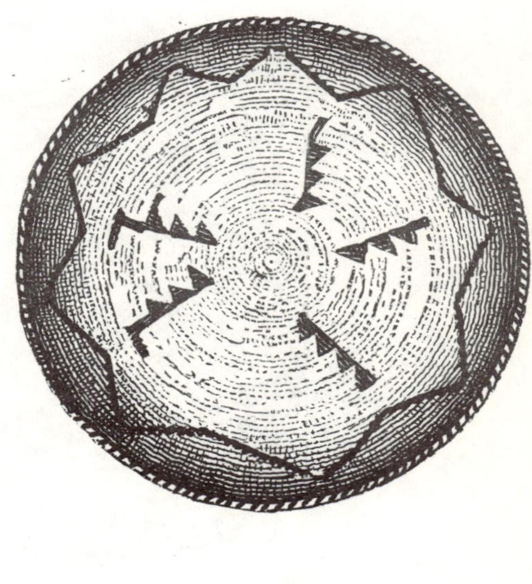

48

FIG. 47. Small coiled mush bowl of the Pai Utes, made by coiling a splint and thin strip of yucca, bast, or osier, and whipping them with split osier. The sewing passes over the two elements of the coil in progress and through the upper element of the coil below, looping always under the subjacent stitches. Ornamentation produced by working into the fabric triangles with strips of martynia or dyed splints. The work is very regular and the texture water-tight, resembling the work of the Apaches and California Indians. The fastening off on the margin is very prettily done by whipping diagonally with two or three threads crossing one another. Collected in Southern Utah, by J. W. Powell, in 1874. Museum number, 14720.

FIG. 48. Coiled dish of Pai Utes. The work is founded upon a wooden plug in the center and coiled by means of an osier and a strip of fiber. Depth, 2¼ inches. The work is neatly done and the ornamentation resembles that of Fig. 47. Collected in Southern Utah, by J. W. Powell, in 1874. Museum number, 14719.

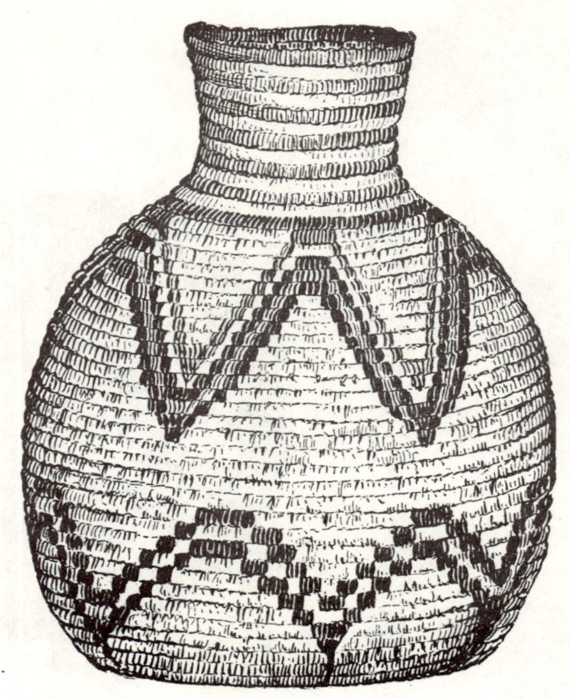

FIG. 49. Water-tight basket bottle of the Apaches. The coiling consists of the rigid osier and soft fiber combination, before mentioned, the latter acting as chinking or calking of the openings. This ware differs essentially from that of the Utes in the glossy even stitches, the care taken in passing them uniformly under the elements of the preceding coil, and the more elaborate shapes and ornamentation. The lines dropped from the bottom of the chevron at the bottom meet in a black spot at the center. The upper chevron and the rings of the neck are in black, red, and yellow splints, alternately. Collected in Arizona, by Dr. J. B. White, U. S. A., in 1875. Museum number, 21494.

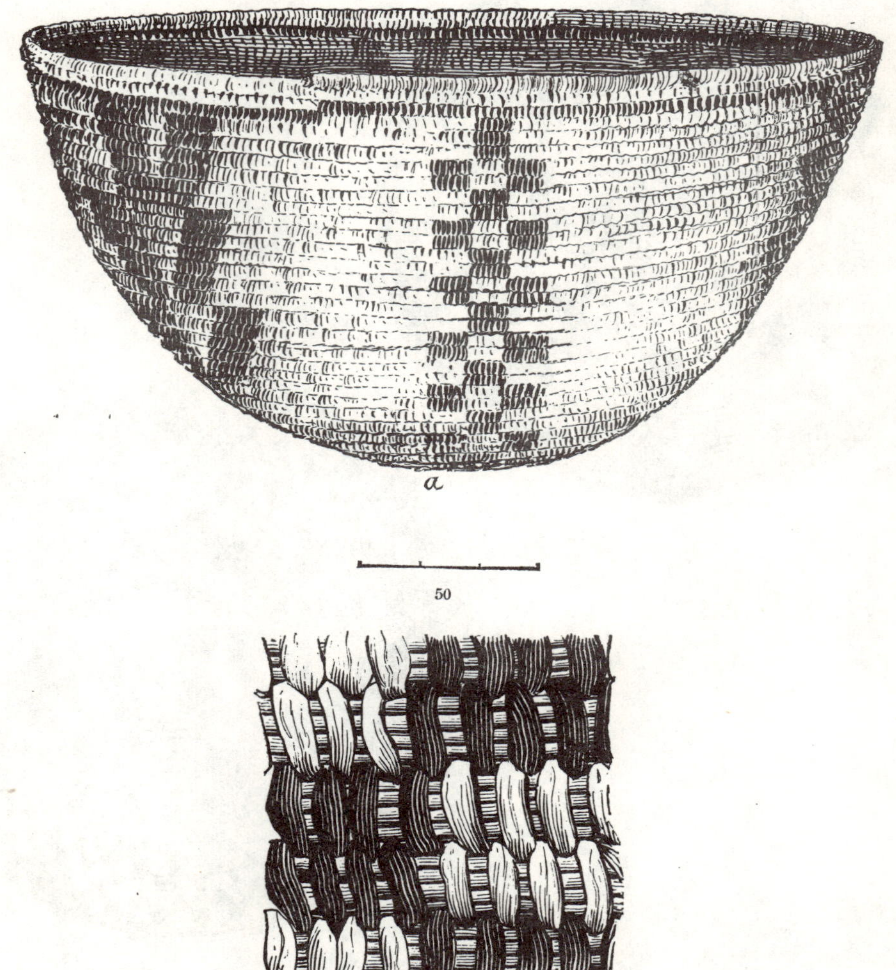

FIG. 50. Coiled basket bowl of the Coahuila Apaches. The coil is a bundle of yucca or other fiber, and the sewing is done with splints of different natural color, resembling reed cane, and with others dyed a beautiful chestnut and black. The lovely cloudy effects produced by the ingenious use of splints of different natural colors resemble those on the Moqui sacred bread trays. The fastening off is simple coil sewing. The ornamentation is a series of crosses arranged vertically, and four series of rhomboids inclosing triangles. Collected in Southern California, by Dr. Edward Palmer. Museum number, 21787.

FIG. 51. One inch of Fig. 50, showing the multiple coil and the method of stitching.

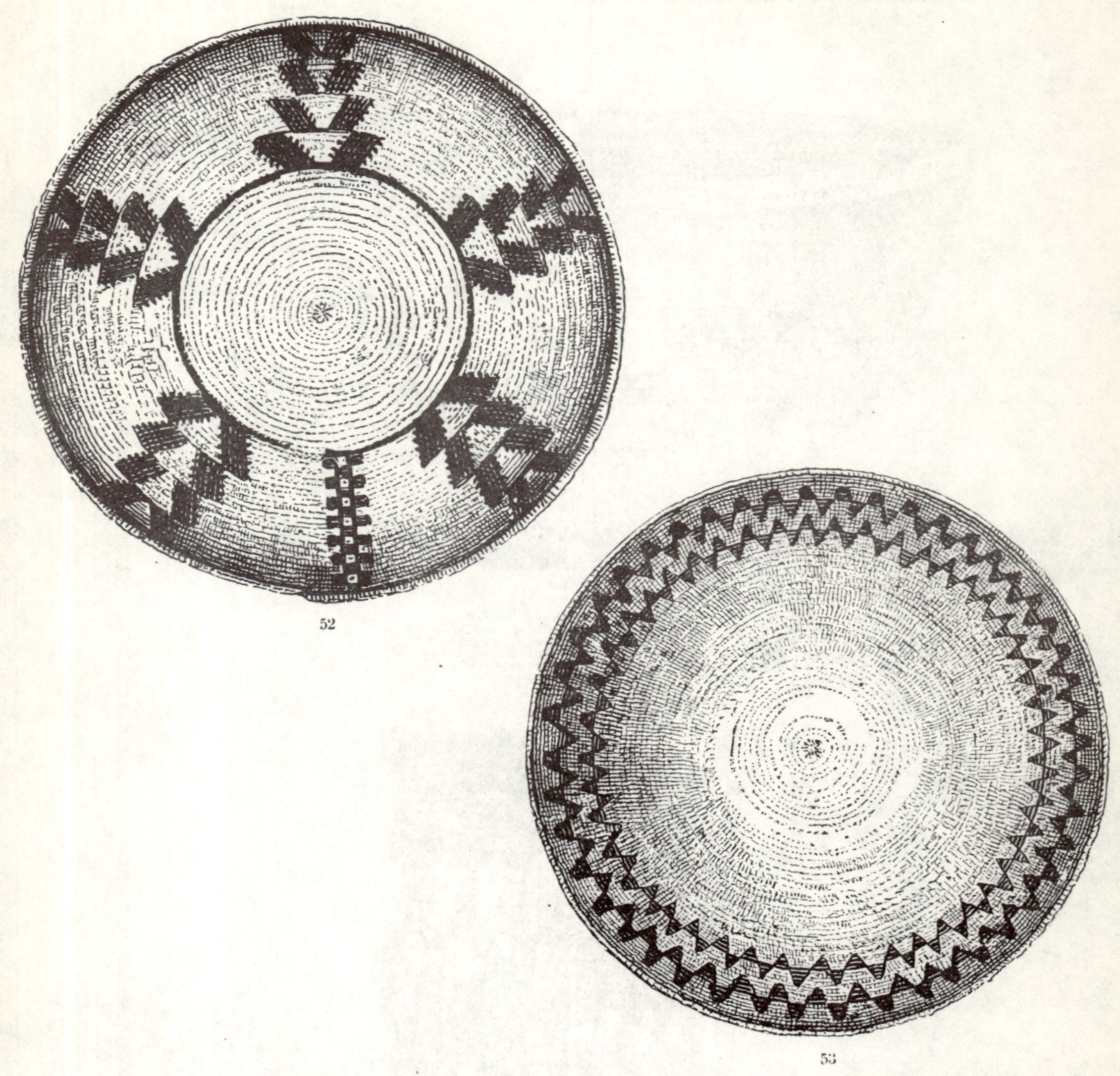

52

53

Fig. 52. Inside view of Fig. 50. The black line at the bottom, nearly continuous, incloses a circle in uniform unvarnished color. All the body color above this line is of a shining yellow, varying in shade. The disposition of the ornament is better shown in this figure.

Fig. 53. A similar Coahuila Apache basket, in which the shading of the body material is in places very dark. The zigzag ornament, effected by the administration of the triangle, is very attractive. Depth, 5½ inches; width, 16 inches. Collected by Dr. Edward Palmer, in Southern California. Museum number, 21786.

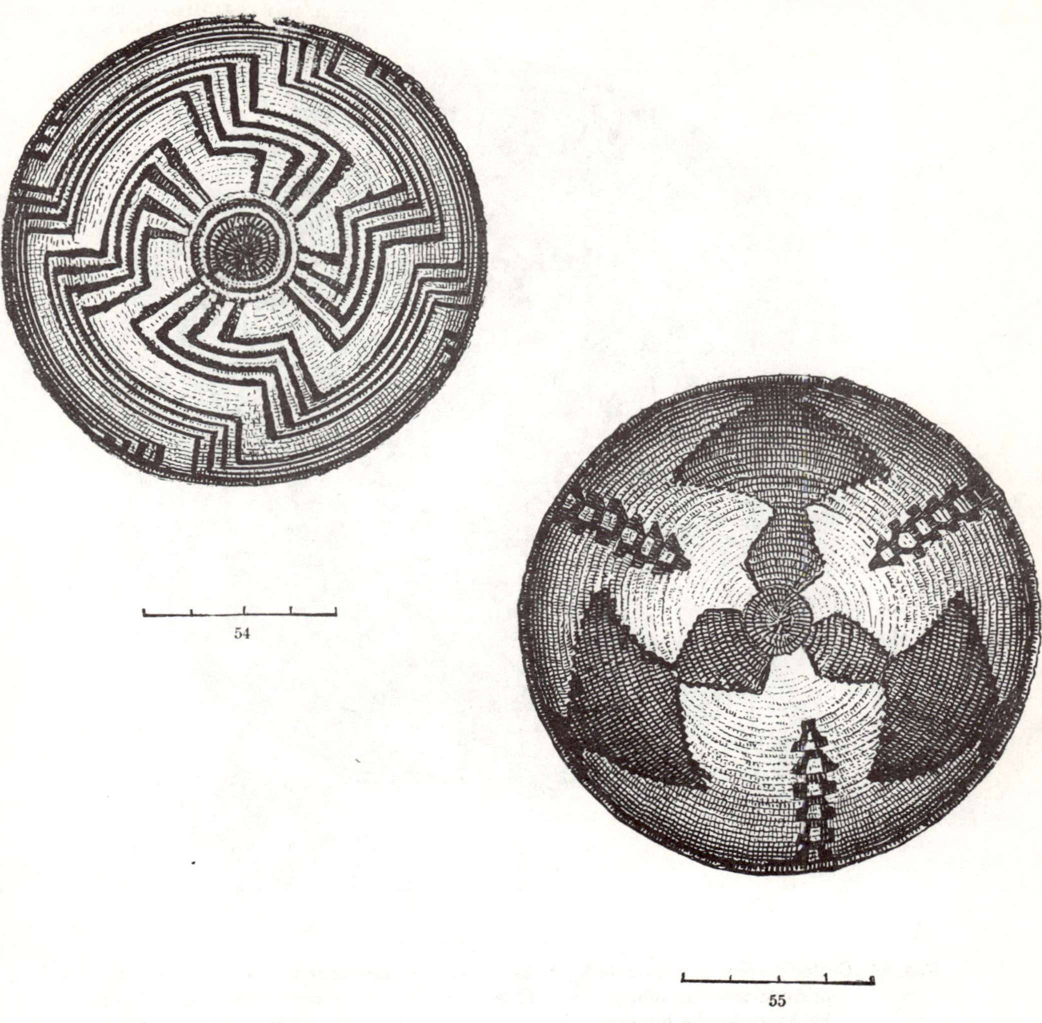

FIG. 54. Coiled osier basket bowl of the Apaches, inside view, made upon a single twig. The apparently unsystematic ornament is indeed very regular. Four lines of black sewing of different lengths proceed from a black ring of the center. From the ends of all these lines sewing is carried to the left in regular curves. Then the four radiating lines are repeated, and the curved lines, until the border is reached. Depth, 4 inches. Collected in Arizona, by Dr. J. B. White. Museum number, 21493.

FIG. 55. Coiled osier basket bowl of the Garotero Apaches, inside view. In every respect this resembles the foregoing. The inclosed triangles alternating with urn patterns constitute the ornamentation. Depth, 3½ inches. Collected on Gila River, by Rev. H. W. Read. Museum number, 4428.

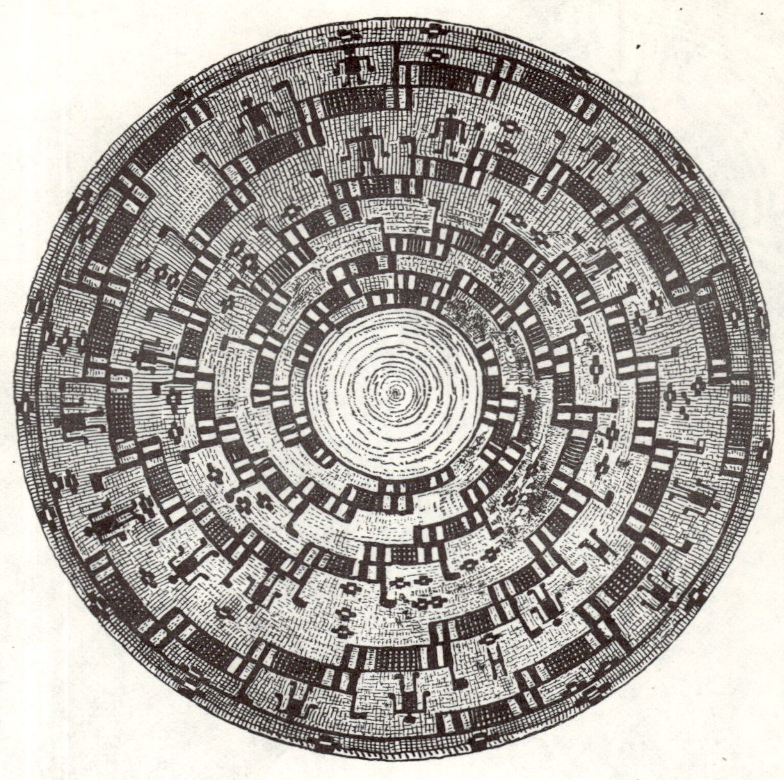

FIG. 56. Coiled basket bowl, made by Yokuts Indians, and here introduced for comparison with Apache work. This is by far the most elaborate piece of basketry in the National Museum. The bottom is plain and flat, bounded by a black line. The body color is that of pine root long exposed; the ornaments are in black, straw color, and brown. To understand this complex figure we must begin at the bottom, where 5 barred parallelograms surround the black ring, with center of brown, and generally four smaller bars of white and black alternating. By a series of steps or gradines this rectangular ornament is carried up to the dark line just below the rim. The spaces in the body color, at first plain, are occupied afterwards by open crosses, and finally by human figures. These human figures are excellent illustrations of the constraining and restraining power of material and environment in human achievement. There are 8 coils and 18 stitches to the inch. Figure, a truncated cone; width, 16½ inches; depth, 7½ inches. Collected in California, by Stephen Powers, in 1875.

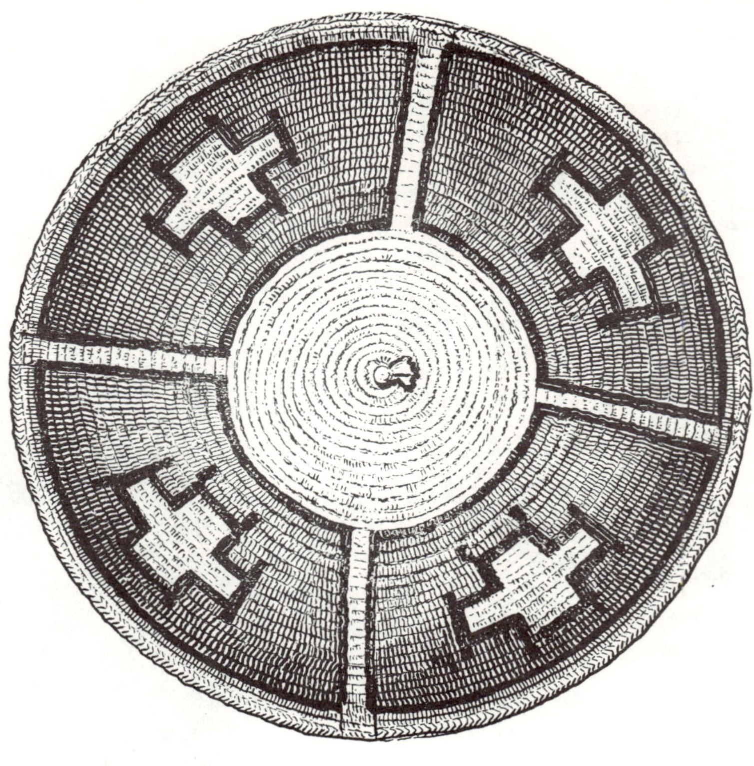

FIG. 57. Coiled basket bowl of the Navajos, with single osier in the coil. Body color natural hue of the wood; ornaments in mahogany-brown, and black. The bowl is divided four quadrants, each separated by a black border and having a cross in the center. The border is very interesting, resembling the braiding on a whip. It is made by sewing with a single splint as follows: The splint is passed under the sewing of the last coil and then drawn over it and backward. It is then passed under again, upward and forward, just in advance of the starting point. Thus, by sewing forward and backward, as one coils a kite string, a braided effect is produced by a single splint thread. Width, 16⅛ inches; depth, 4½ inches. Collected in New Mexico, in 1873, by Governor Arny. Museum number, 16510.

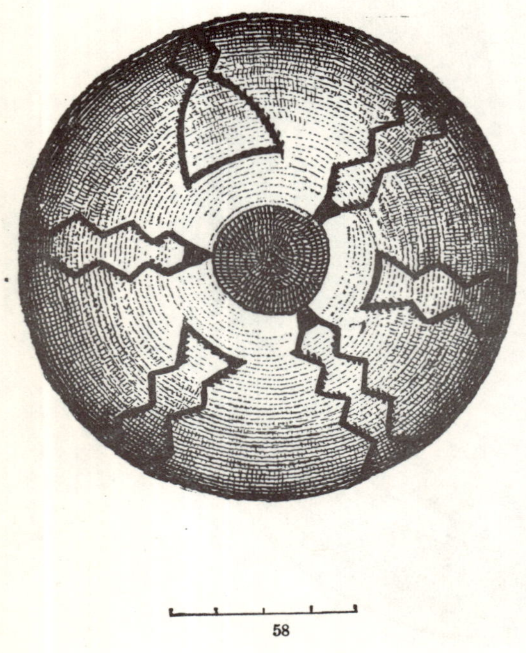

58

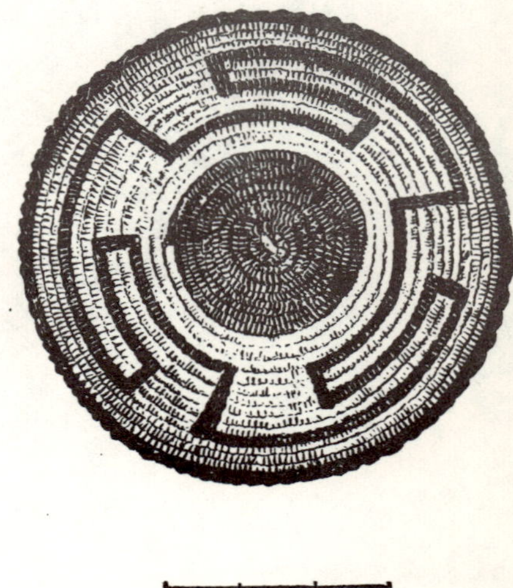

59

FIG. 58. Coiled basket bowl of the Pimas, made up on a foundation of yucca, the sewing done with splints of willow or pine. The rude character of the ornament is worthy of notice. Depth, 4 inches. Collected by Dr. Edward Palmer, in Arizona. Museum number, 5548.

FIG. 59. Coiled basket bowl of the Pimas, similar in structure to 58. The grecque ornament is wrought in with tolerable symmetry. The border has the braided appearance before mentioned, given by forward and backward sewing along the border with a single splint. In this instance the stitch passes backward three stitches of the sewing each time. This is truly the most ingenious and effective work of the kind yet seen. Collected by Mrs. Georgia Stout, Pima Agency, Arizona. Museum number, 27837.

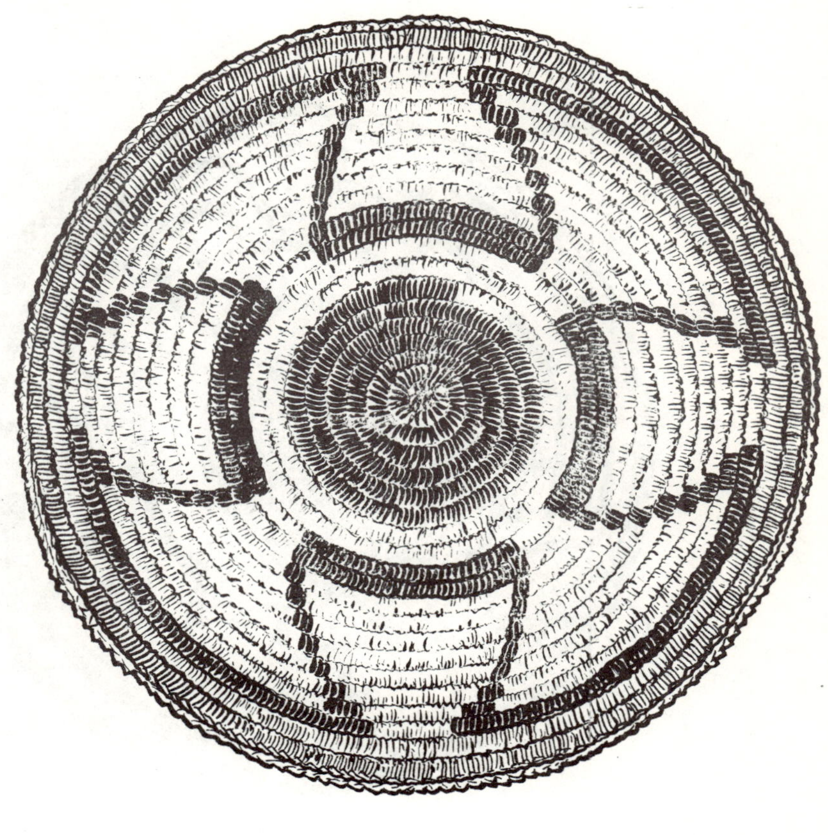

FIG. 60. Coiled basket bowl of the Pimos, built on yucca fiber and sewed with rhus or willow. The ornamentation is in red paint and splints dyed black. The border is back and forward sewing to imitate a braid. The method of administration is quite apparent in the specimen. The border stitches have an excursion varying from 2 to 4 of the regular stitches of the last coil at the top of the bowl. Depth, 3 inches. Collected in Arizona, by Dr. E. Palmer. Museum number, 76038.

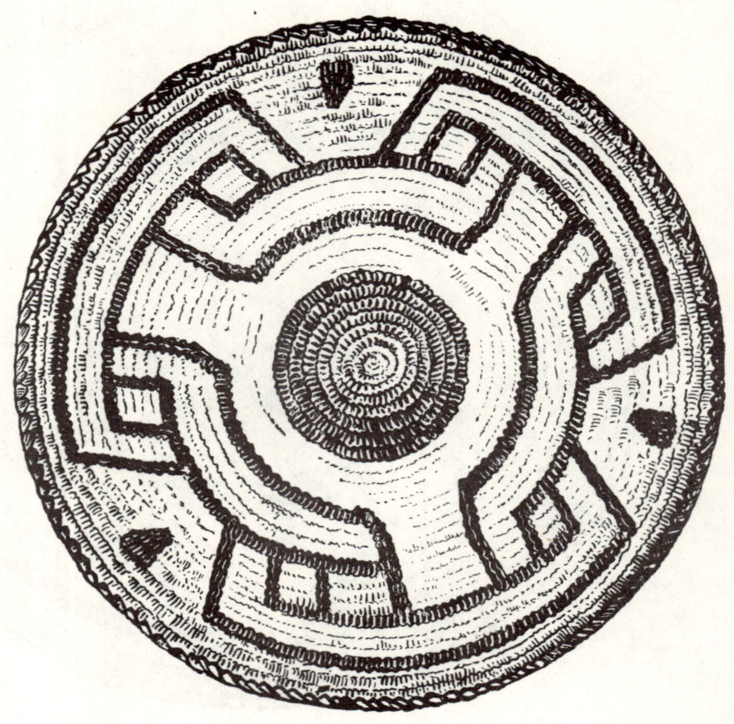

FIG. 61. Coiled basket bowl of Pimos. Made on yucca with splint sewing similar to those just described. The ornament is evidently the work of a beginner, but the pattern is both regular and unique, all the parts being in threes and the two sides of each pattern quite symmetrical. Border of backward and forward sewing, quite uniform in appearance, but done regardless of the number of body stitches beneath. Width, 8 inches; depth, 2¼ inches. Collected in Arizona, by Dr. Edward Palmer, in 1884. Museum number, 76039.

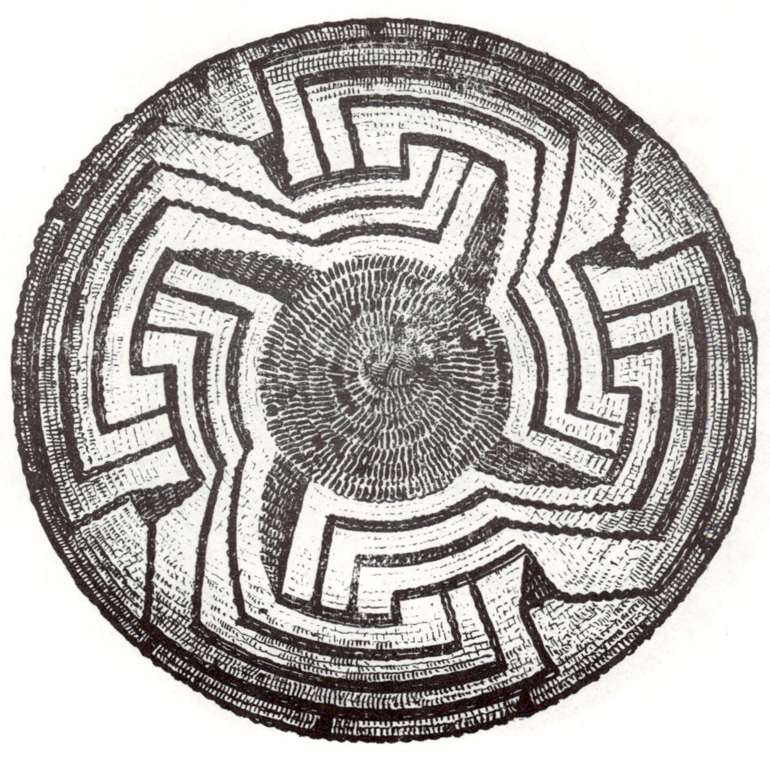

FIG. 62. Coiled basket bowl of Pimos, flat-bottomed. The ornament consists of four similar patterns, based on four elongated right-angled triangles. Each of the other lines of the pattern is as nearly parallel to one of the sides of this triangle as the texture will permit. It is difficult to conceive how this design was studied out beforehand. Width, 12¼ inches; height, 5 inches. Collected in Arizona, in 1884, by Dr. E. Palmer. Museum number, 76040.

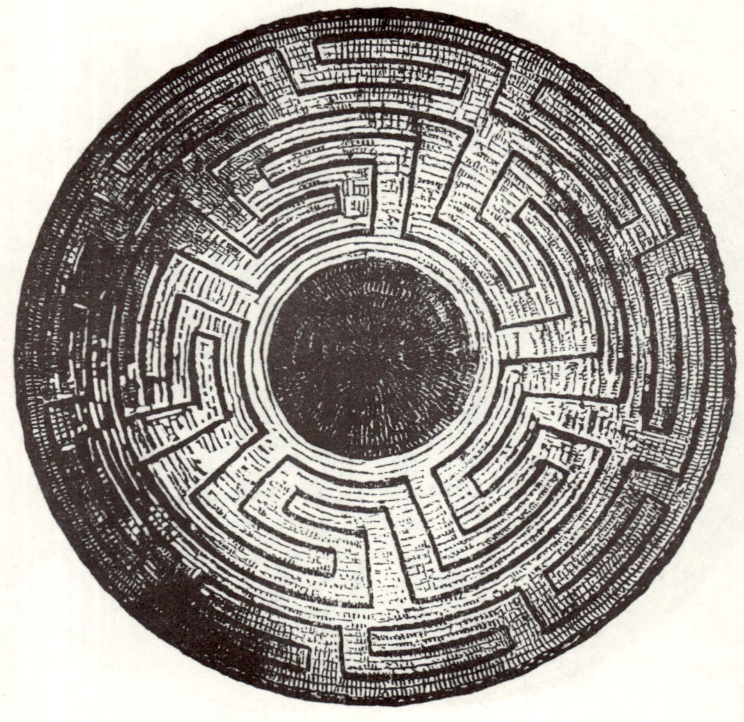

FIG. 63. Large basket bowl of Pimos. The manufacture is similar to that in those just mentioned, but the use of the continuous fret in ornamentation is remarkable, as exhibiting the easy manner in which the fret may have arisen in basketry. The border is a false braid formed by a single splint and resembles an elongated guilloche. Width, 18¾; depth, 5¼. Collected in Arizona, by Dr. E. Palmer, in 1874. Museum number, 76041.

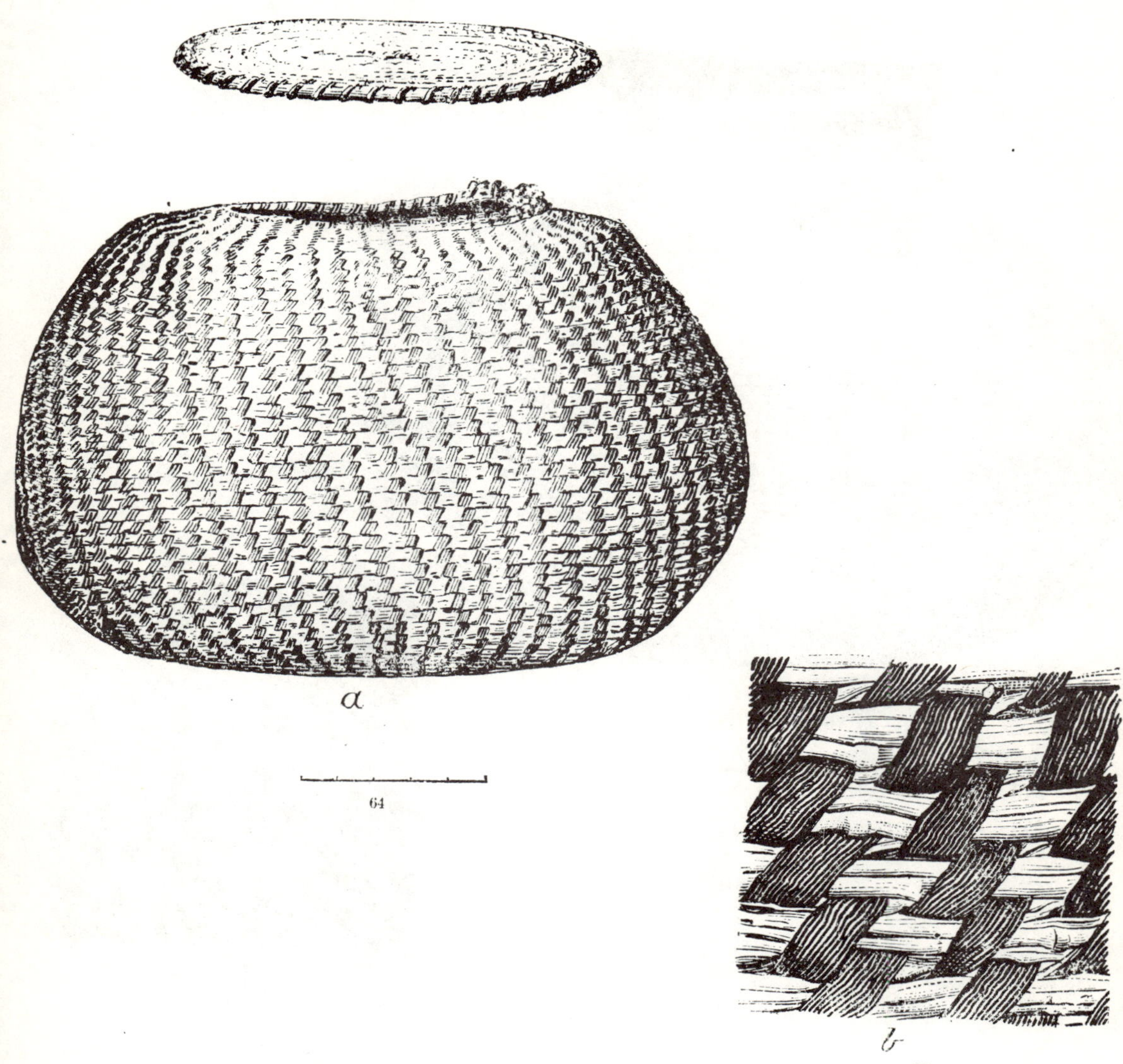

FIG. 64. Small twined granary of straw, made by Pimos. Made of wheat-straw in a coil sewed with bands of willow-bark. The very noticeable feature about this specimen is that only in a few cases do the stitches of the coils interlock. Diameter, 20 inches; height, 12 inches. Collected in Arizona, by Dr. E. Palmer, in 1884.

FIG. 65. One square inch of 64, showing the coiled straws and the method of sewing.

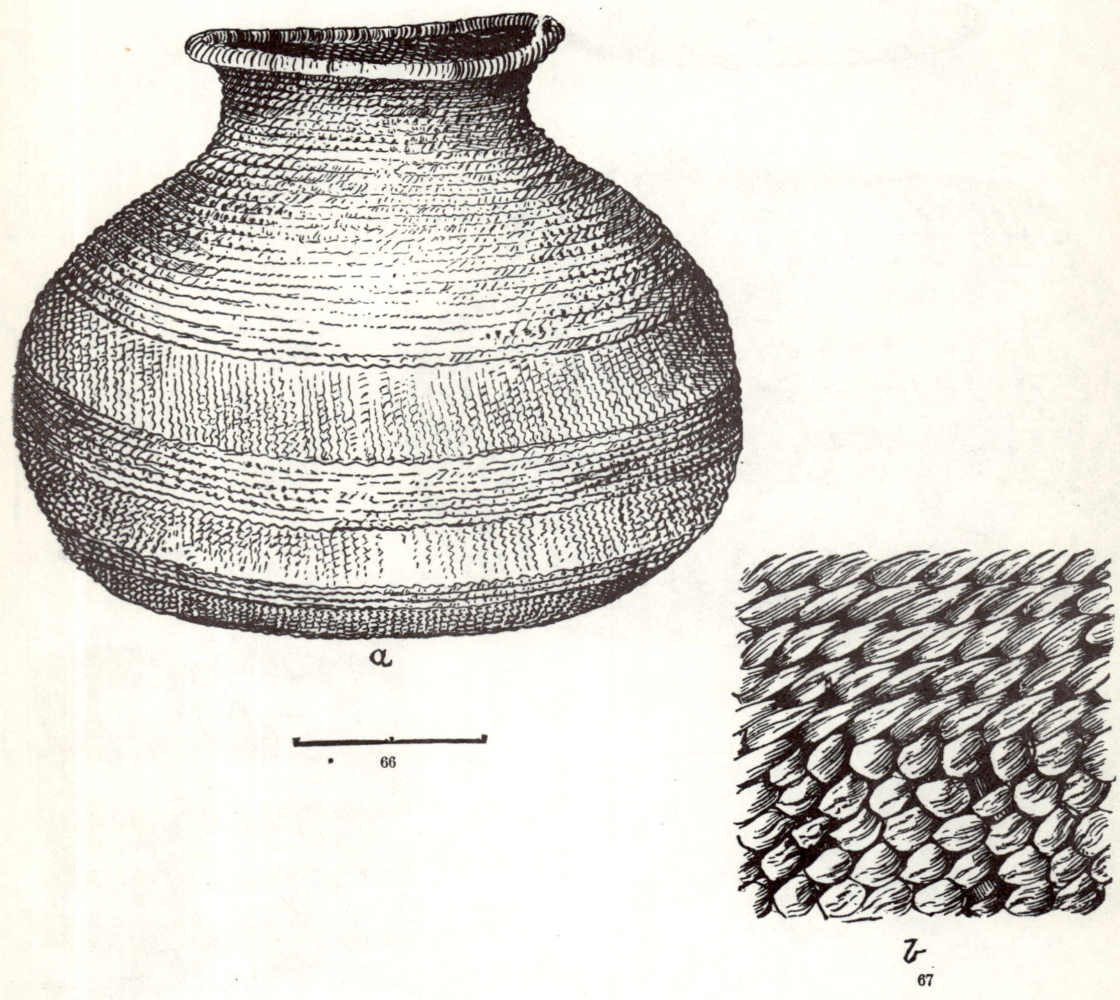

FIG. 66. Twined jar-shaped basket of the Mokis. Excepting in the rigid material and the pottery form, we have here all the details of the west coast basketry. At the center of the bottom each twining includes two warp twigs; the next round the same plan is followed, but the stitches alternate. This for 10 rows; on the fifth is an exterior twining for ornament. Then succeed 6 rows of twining on each twig, then 4 rows of twining over two twigs, then 9 rows of single twining overlaid by two double rows of external twining. The rest of the surface is covered with twining over every warp twig, onoverlaid the upper portion and at the bulge by external twining. The fastening off is mere whipping. Collected in Moki pueblos in Arizona, by J. W. Powell, in 1884.

FIG. 67. One inch of 66, showing the twining on single and on double rods.

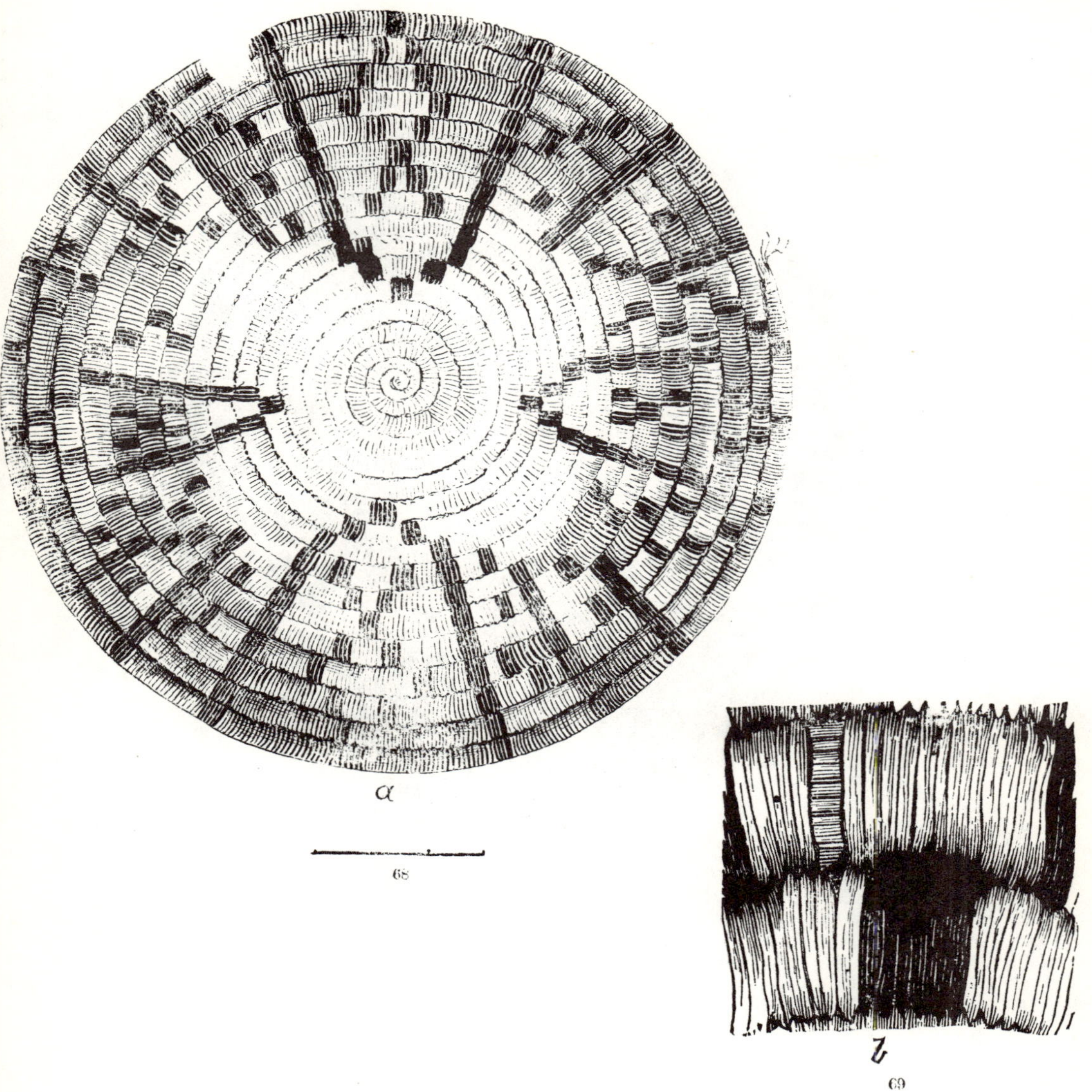

FIG. 68. Coiled sacred meal tray of the Mokis. A bunch of yucca leaf stems, or of grass, varying from ½ inch to 1 inch in diameter, is sewed in a continuous coil by means of slender threads of yucca fiber about $\frac{1}{16}$th inch in width, and very uniform throughout. Each stitch of the progressing coil is caught into a stitch of the coil beneath with perfect regularity, forming a dish looking like a great worm coiled up. The ornamentation is in yellow and brown. The first spots interiorly contain from 4 to 6 stitches. On the next turn a series is arranged with relation to these. By the simple management of this device hundreds of patterns are worked out. Collected in Arizona by J. W. Powell.

FIG. 69. One square inch of Fig. 68, showing the method of administration.

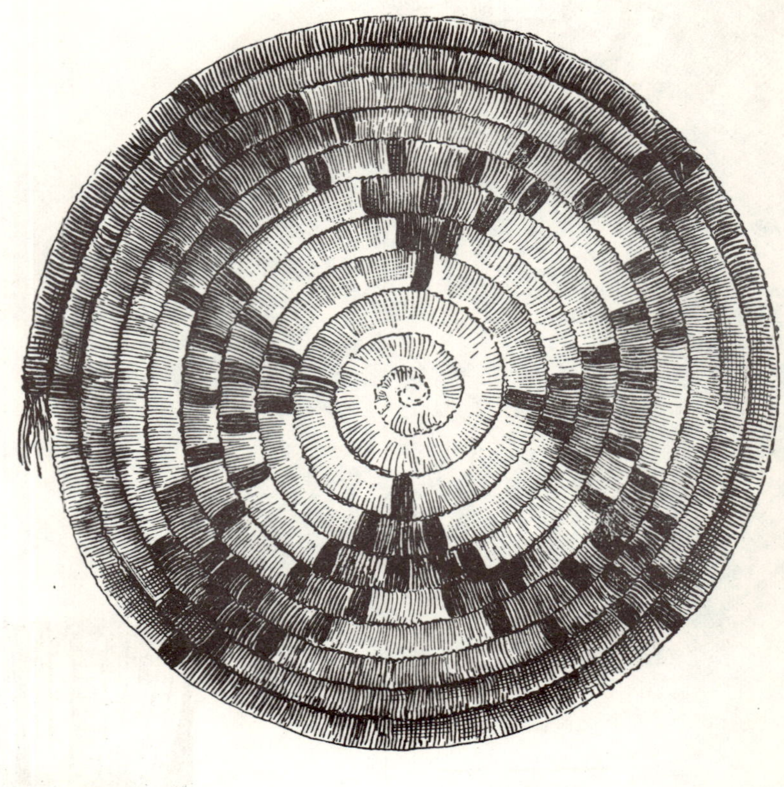

FIG. 70. Coiled sacred meal tray of the Mokis. The coloring of the interior exhibits the fine shading produced by the skillful manipulation of the dark and the light side of the fiber. Collected in Arizona, by J. W. Powell.

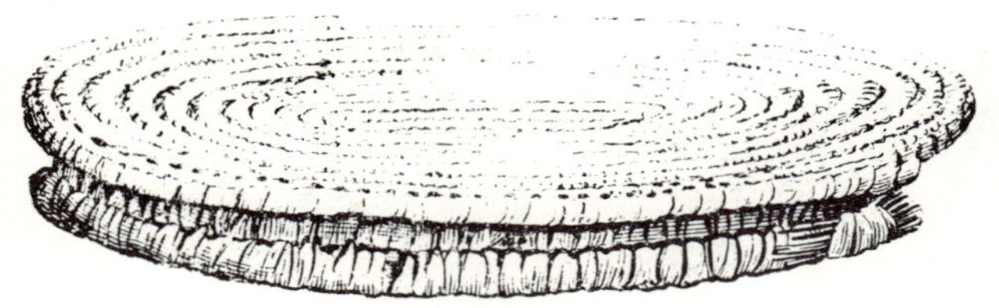

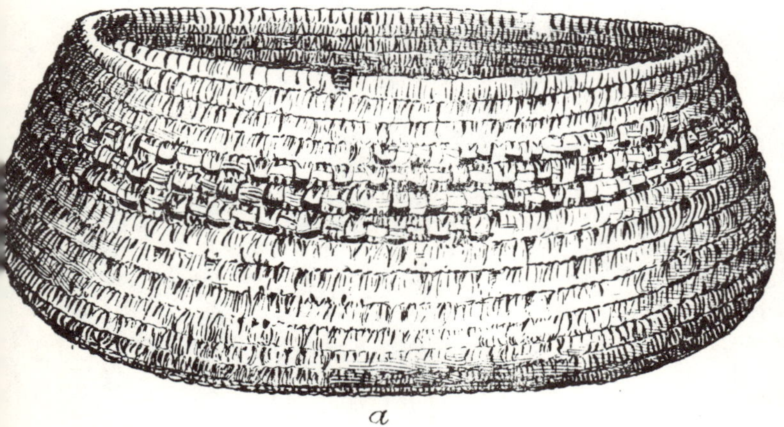

a

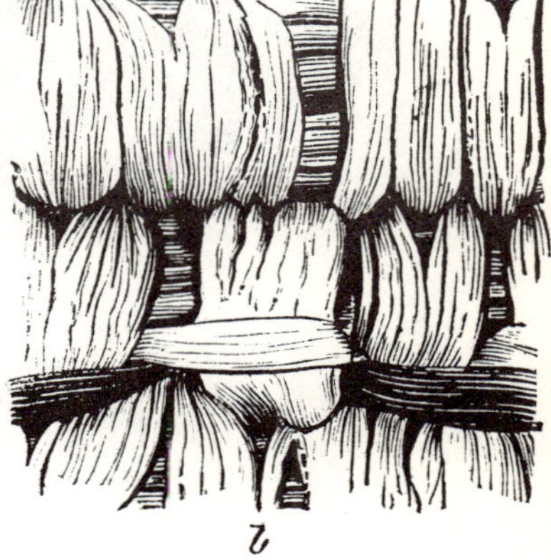

b

72

FIG. 71. Coiled basket of Upper Egypt, made of bundles of palm-leaf veins, sewed with strips of palm leaf. Introduced here for comparison with the Moki work. Ornamentation in red and black. A long red or black strip of leaf is laid on the outside of a coil and caught down by alternate stitches. The varying of the number of stitches caught over or covered by these strips produces a multitude of effects. These baskets are frequently pitched for boats or Moses' arks. Collected by Dr. G. W. Samson, in Upper Egypt, 1848. Museum number, 74871.

FIG. 72. One square inch of Fig. 71, showing the sewing and the strips of ornament.

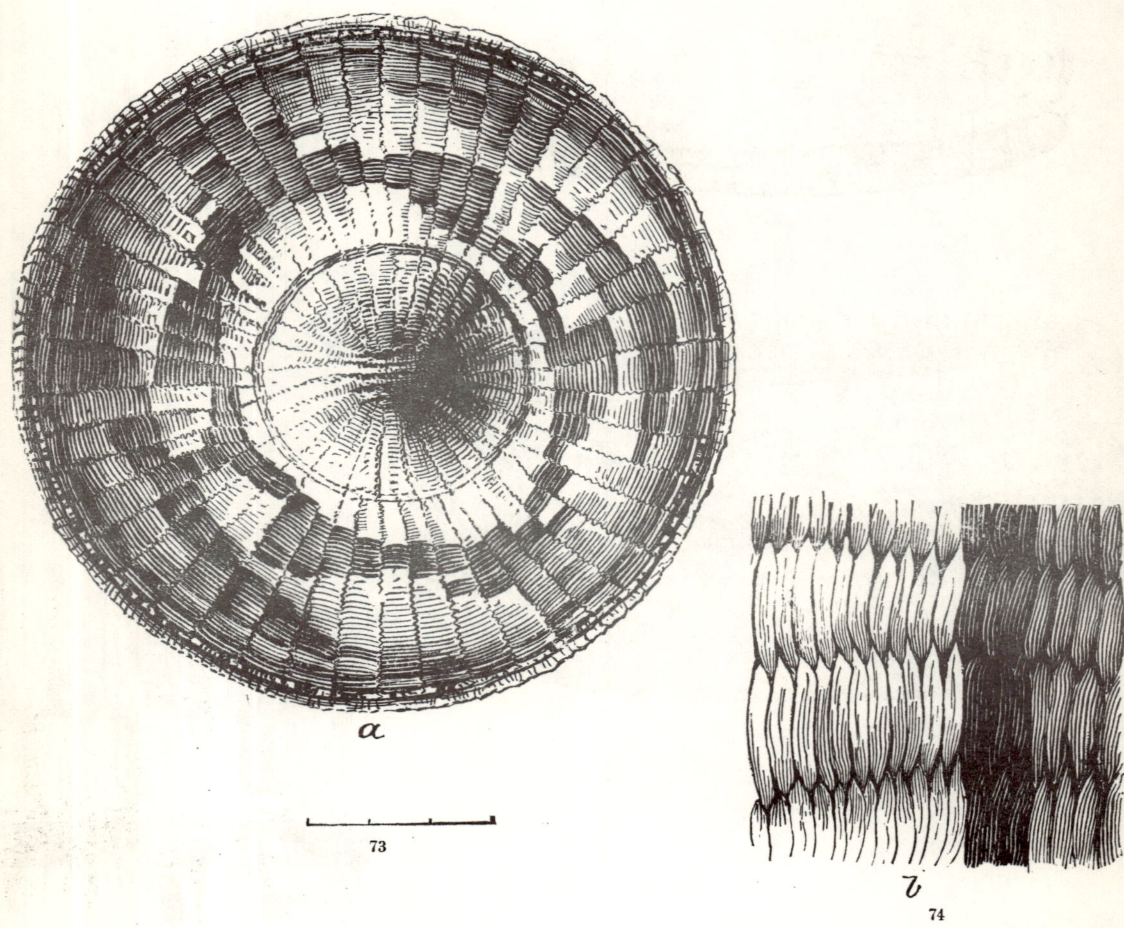

FIG. 73. Woven bread-tray of the Mokis, made upon radiating warp twigs by weaving bits of colored twig, stripped of their bark, in and out, and by fastening off the ends alongside of the warp twigs inside the fabric. This type should be particularly noticed as the first example yet encountered of the regular basket weaving so common in the ware of more civilized peoples. Some of the bits of twig used are less than an inch long, and none of them ever exceed a foot. The figure is the same on both sides, but each stitch and design in front is just one space farther to the right on the back. Collected in Arizona, by J. W. Powell, in 1874.

FIG. 74. One square inch of Fig. 73, showing the regularity and disposition of the weaving.

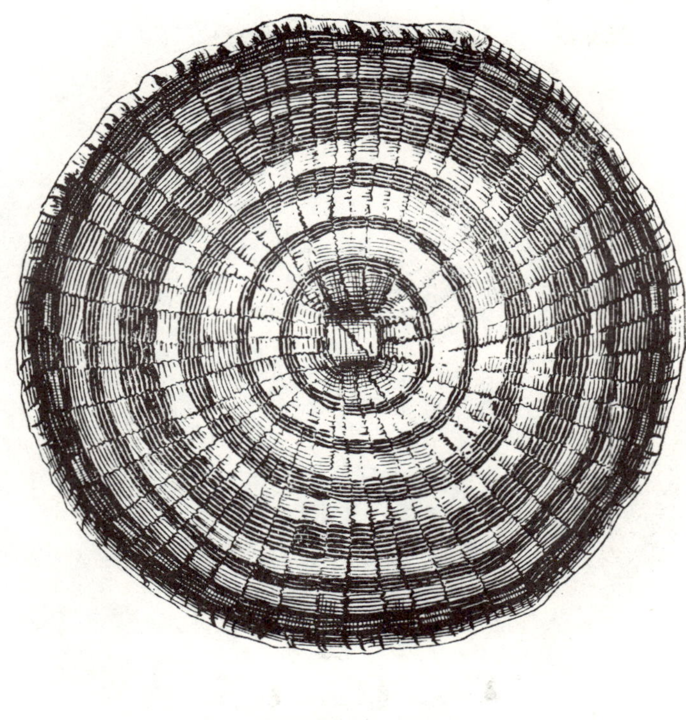

FIG. 75. Woven bread-tray of the Mokis, similar in workmanship to Fig. 73. The fastening off is done by whipping one or two twigs around the edge by means of yucca fiber. The design is a series of concentric rings in pretty colors, the figures corresponding exactly on the two sides. Collected in Arizona, by J. W. Powell, 1874.

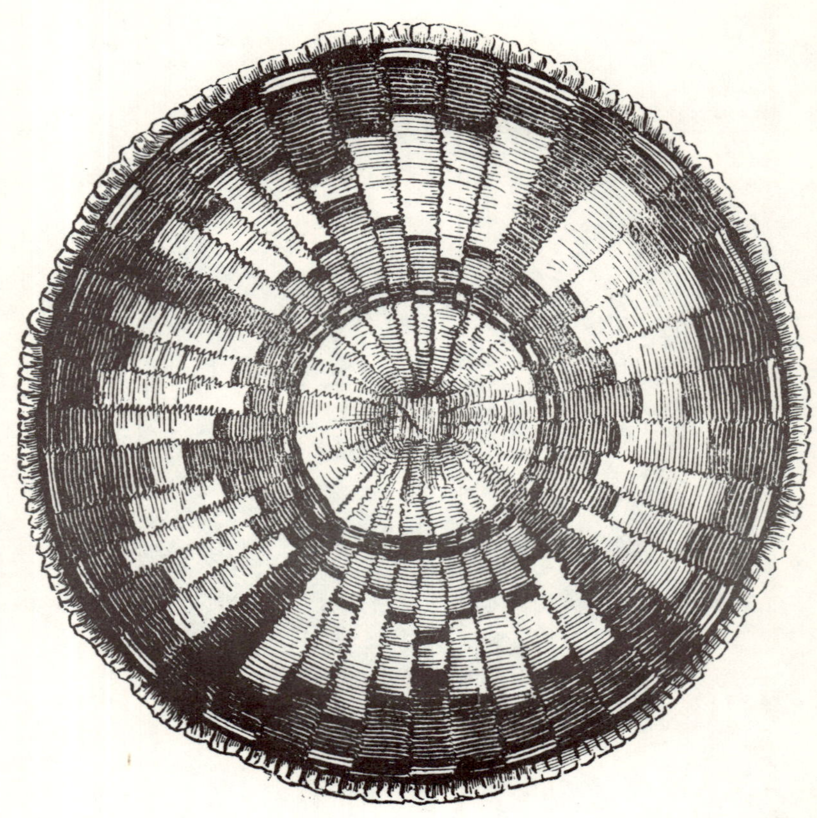

FIG. 76. Woven basket-tray of the Mokis. This figure shows very clearly what pleasing designs may be worked out by the skillful adjustment of simple forms and color. In the bright colors used for this ware the Mokis produce decidedly brilliant effects. Collected in Arizona, by J. W. Powell, in 1874.

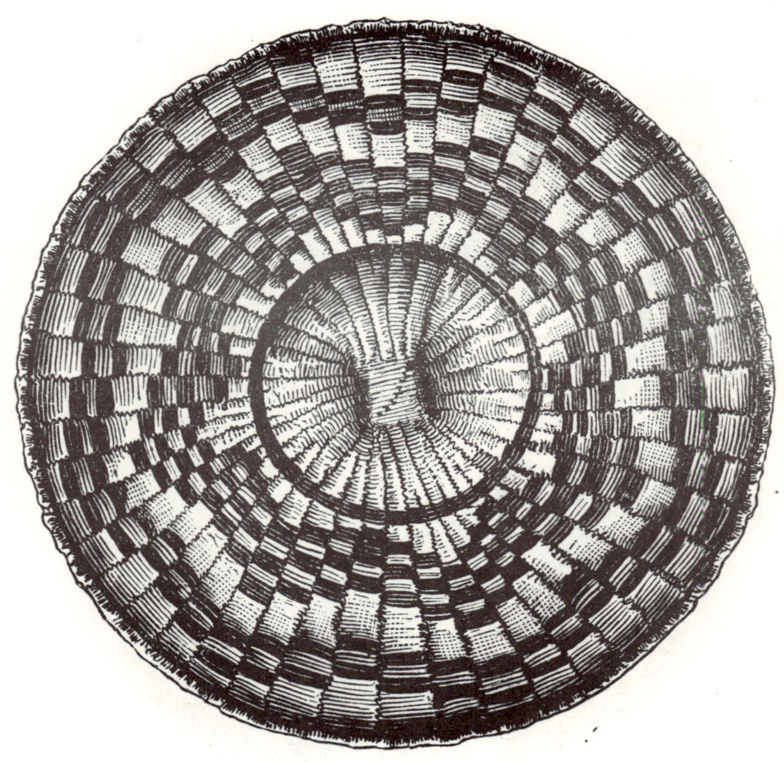

FIG 77. Woven basket-tray of the Mokis. In this figure should be noticed the method of starting the weaving. A certain number of twigs are plaited at the center into a cross. These twigs are spread out so as to form the radii of a circle, and the little twigs are so woven as to increase the length of the meshes going outward. Here and there an additional warp twig is introduced at points where they are needed, but not beyond the dark circle. The ornamentation in this case is produced simply by the use of patches, two or three stitches of the same color alternating with the body color. Collected in Arizona, by J. W. Powell, in 1874.

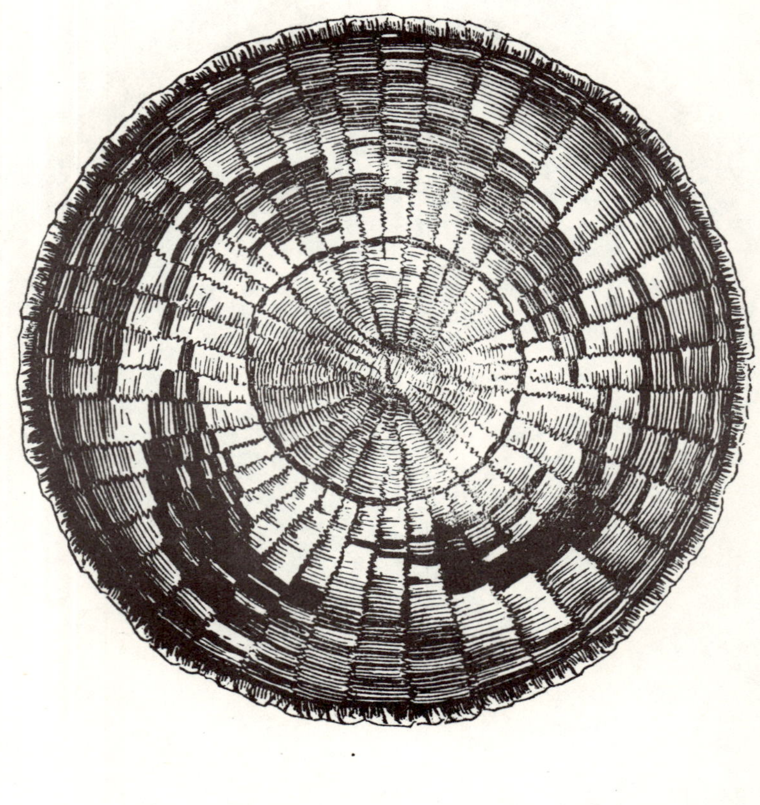

FIG. 78. Woven basket-tray of the Mokis. The especial attraction about this specimen is the genuine cloud effects produced on the surface by the simplest means. This represents a stage of art far above the genius of savage culture. Collected in Arizona, by J. W. Powell, in 1874.

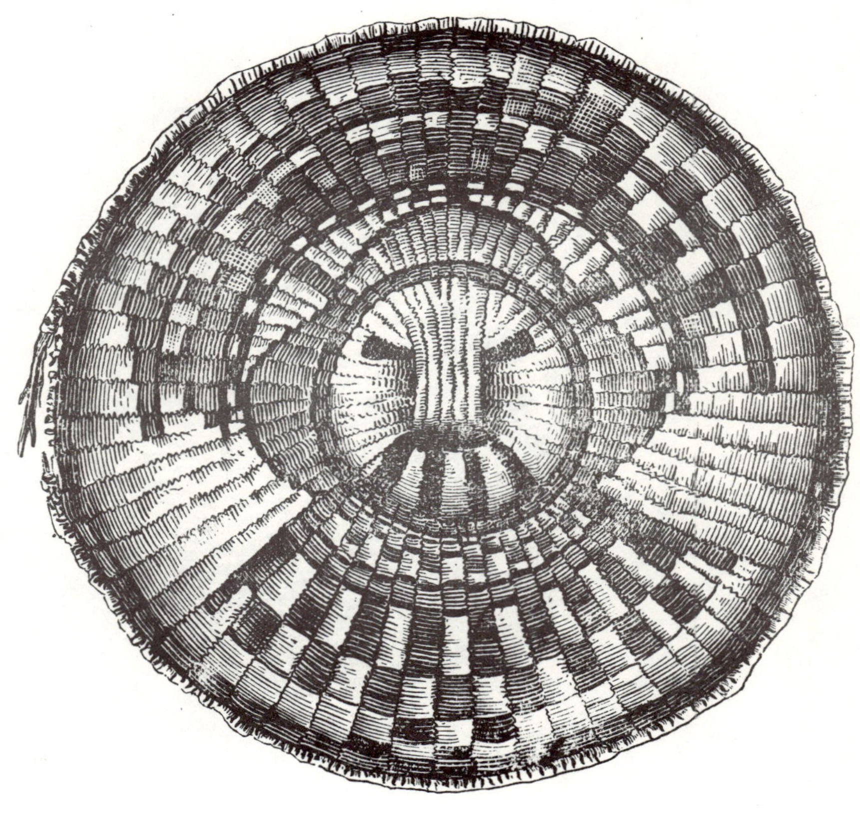

FIG. 79. Woven basket-tray of the Mokis, made as others just described. The very insecure method of fastening off is shown on the left rim. The pattern on this specimen introduces no new elements or colors. The elaborate human head, with brilliant cape and gorgeous head-dress, reminds one of Aztec inscriptions. Collected in Arizona, by J. W. Powell, 1874.

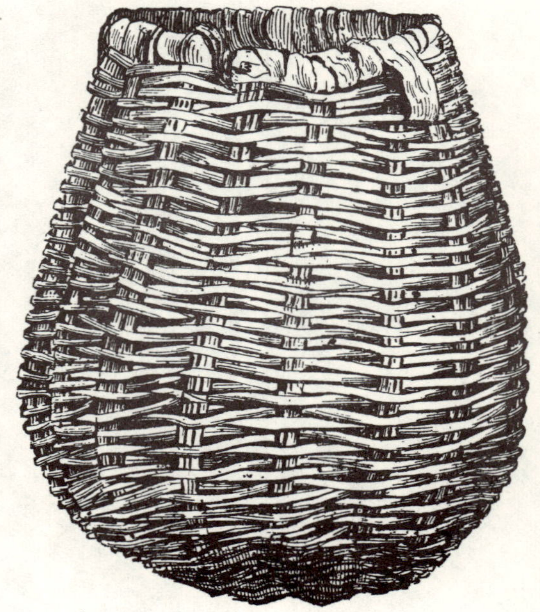

FIG. 80. Woven peach-basket of the Zuñis. More than the Moki trays, this specimen recalls the method of manufacture to be seen in the thousands of baskets employed in civilized drudgery. Roughness, asymmetry, rude fastening off with yucca fiber are its attractions. Collected in New Mexico, by J. W. Powell. Museum number, 40291.

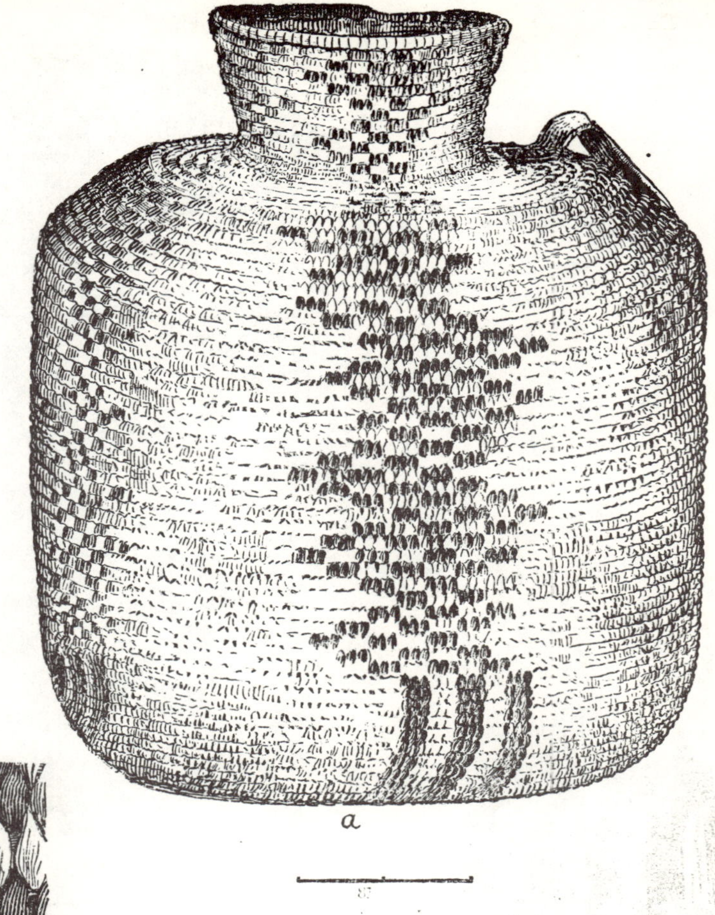

82

Fig. 81. Jar-shaped coiled basket from Zuñi Indians. This is a very beautiful specimen of coiled ware for this region, in shape, regularity of stitch, and ornamentation in black. Upon the authority of explorers the text is made to say that the pottery-making Indians are not good basket-makers. This specimen looks as though it might have come from California. Collected in New Mexico by J. W. Powell, in 1874.

Fig. 82. One square inch of 81, showing the use of the strip of fiber for chinking, and the alternation of white and black stitches.

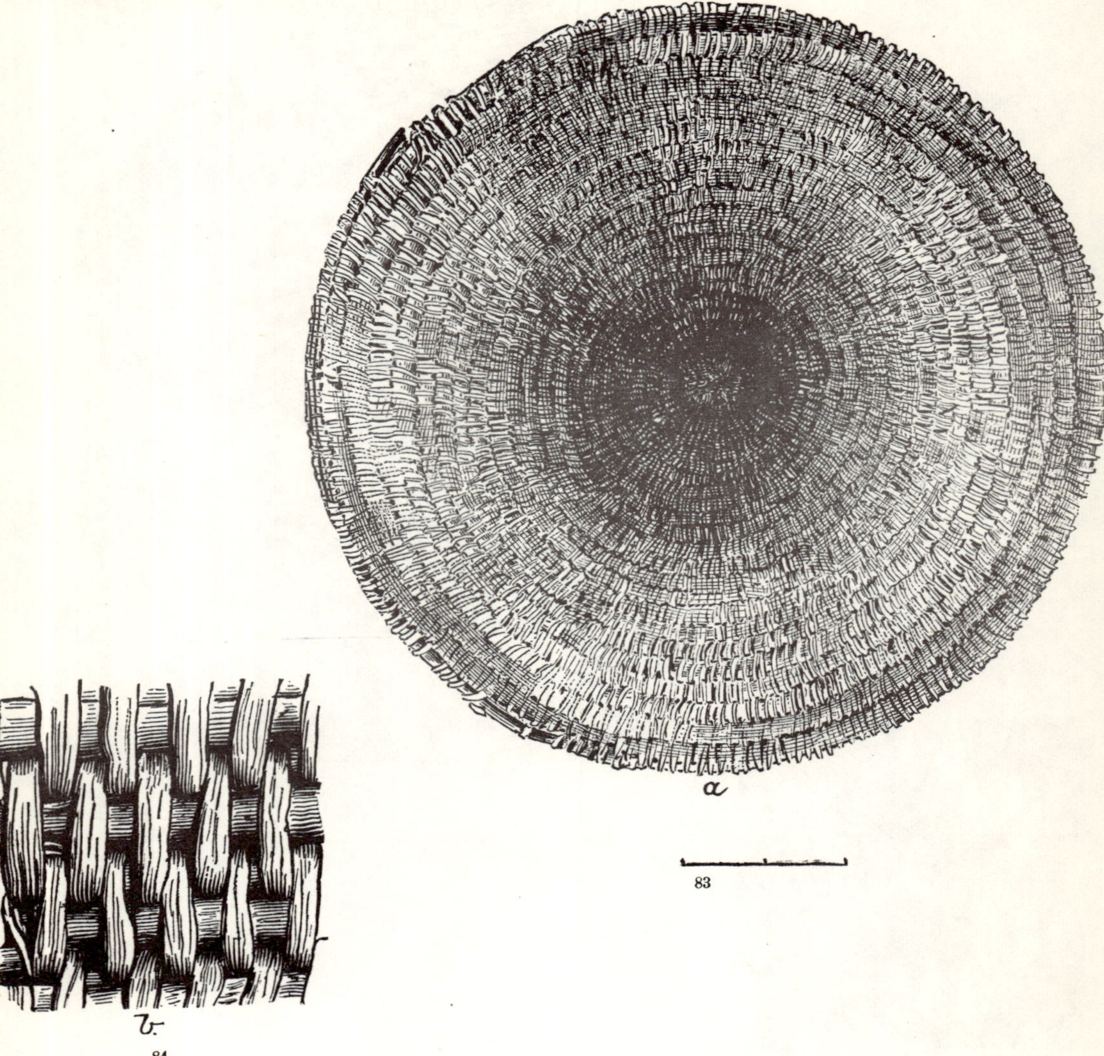

Fig. 83. Coiled basket-tray from Zuñi. The texture is exceedingly open, owing to the use of the single rod in the coil with coarse chinking. Collected in New Mexico, by J. W. Powell, in 1874.

Fig. 84. One square inch of Fig. 83, showing the warp rods and the method of sewing. This stitch is best employed in the exquisite rattan baskets of Siam.

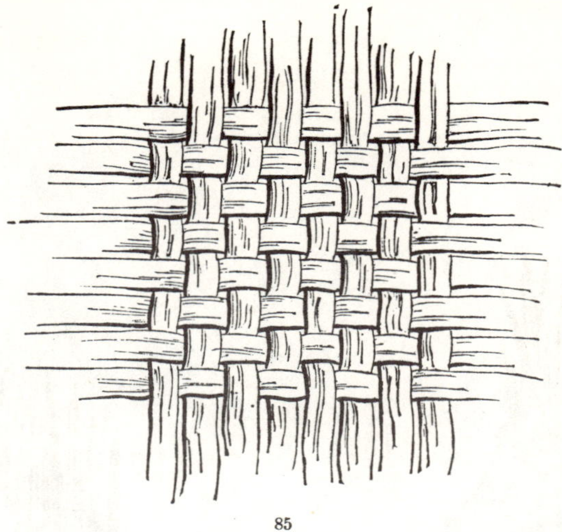

85

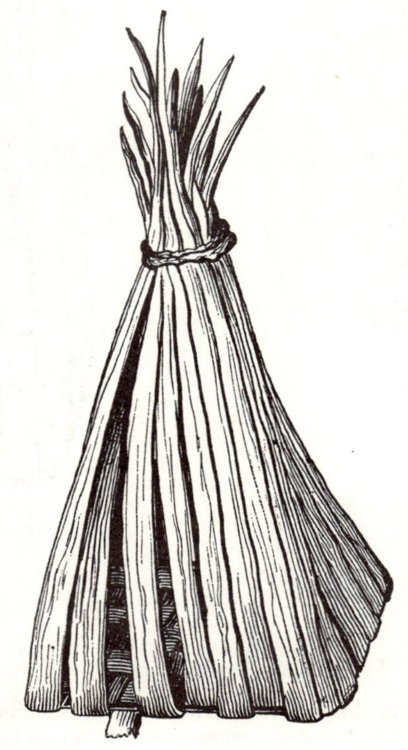

86

Fig. 85. The first step in ordinary basket-weaving, showing how the bottom is set up in split cane or splints of tough wood.

Fig. 86. The second step in basket-weaving, showing how the bottom splints are turned up to form the sides.

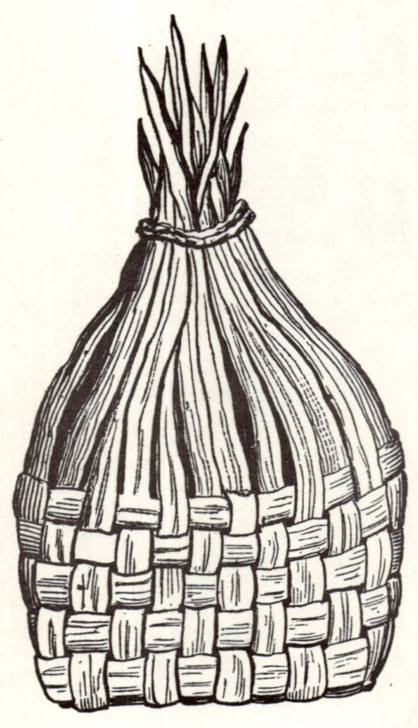

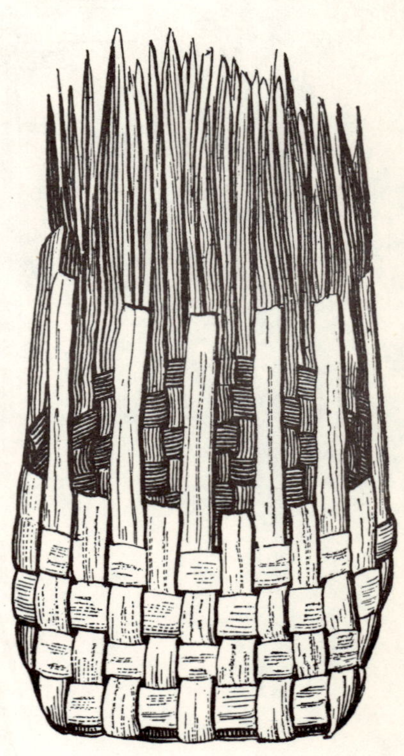

FIGS. 87, 88. Showing the method of completing the weaving on the sides of an ordinary splint basket, and preparing to lay on the rim.

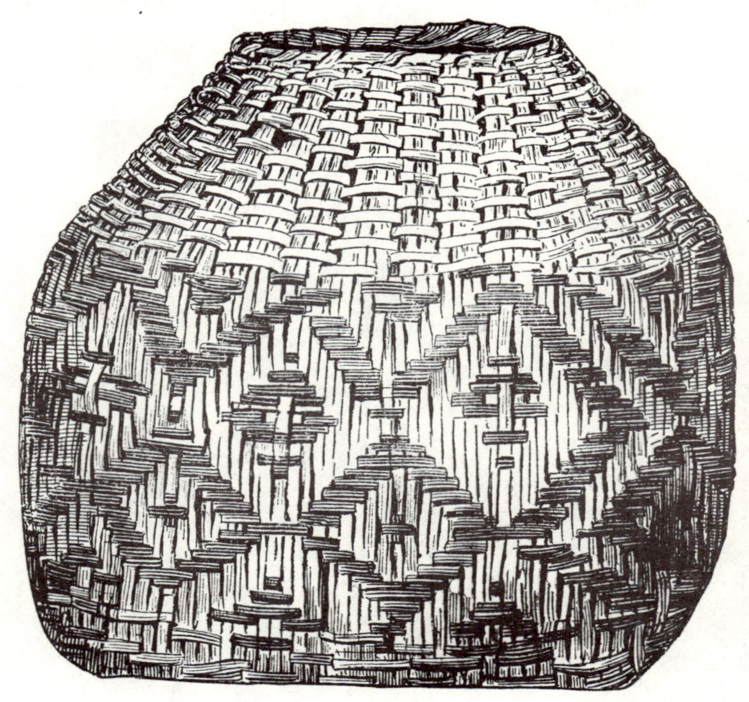

FIG. 89. Twilled woven basket, covered with diaper pattern below, made from cane, by Cherokee Indians. Similar ware is produced by all our southern Indians. The diaper pattern is produced by overlapping two or more warp sticks with each stitch. Collected in North Carolina, by Dr. Edward Palmer, in 1880.

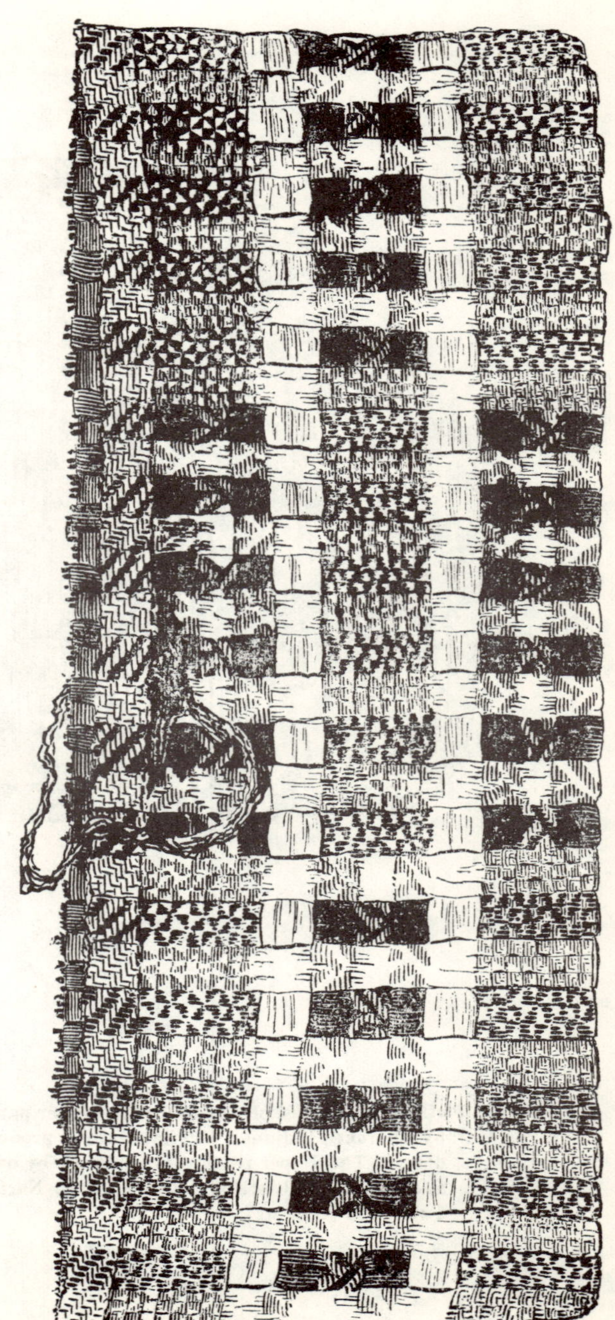

FIG. 90. Twilled palm-leaf basket-wallet of Fiji Islanders, woven double, the inside of plain checker pattern of broad pieces. The exterior covered with every conceivable manipulation of black and white strips of palm-leaf, varying in width. Introduced here for comparison with twilled weaving on our continent. Collected in Fiji, by Captain Wilkes, in 1840.

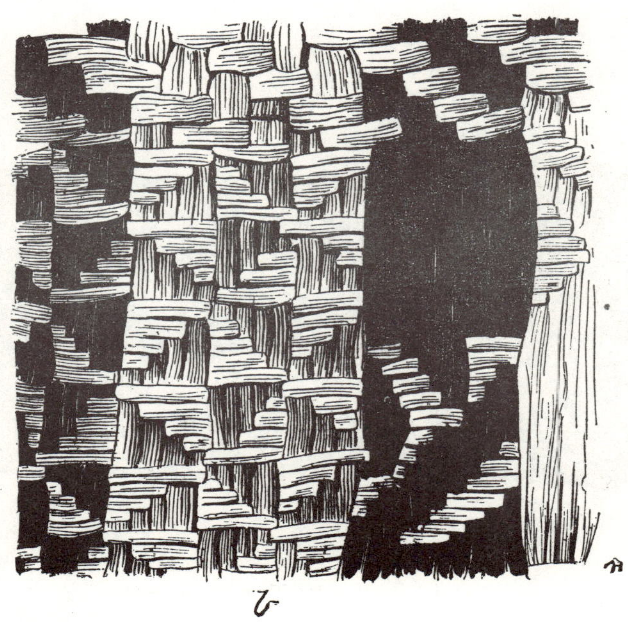

FIG. 91. One square inch of 90 enlarged to show the method of cross-stitching in Fiji basketry, combined with varying width of strips.

PLATE LVI.

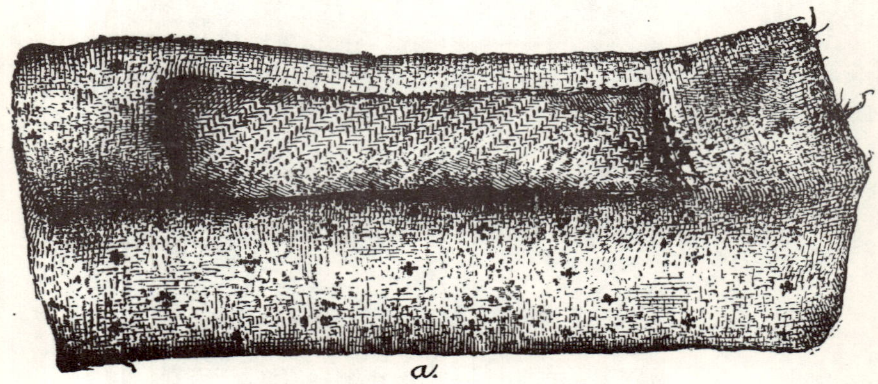

FIG. 92. Woven fish-basket of Fiji Islanders. This specimen is also woven double, the inside being very coarse. Collected in Fiji Islands, in 1840, by Captain Wilkes.

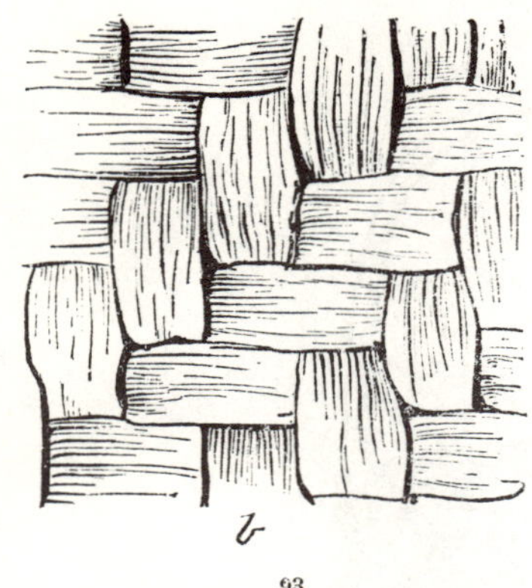

93

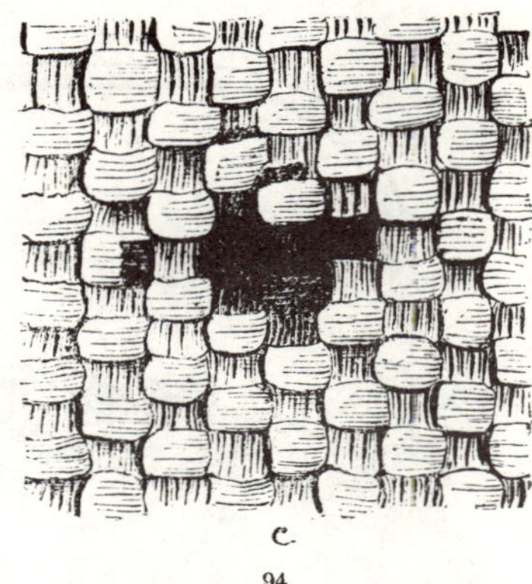

94

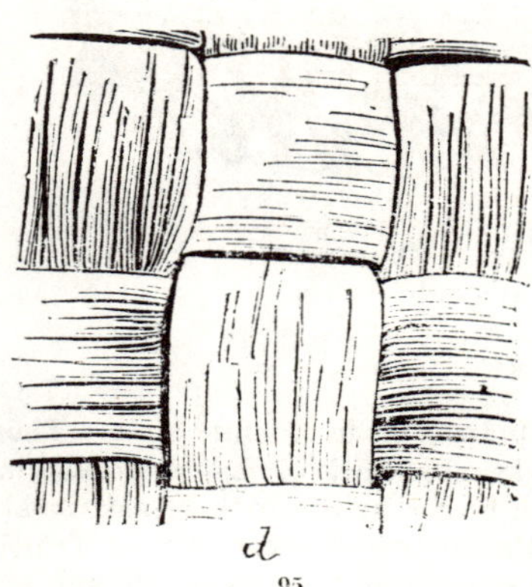

95

Fig. 93. One inch of the bottom of 92 enlarged to show the simple twilled weaving.

Fig. 94. Plain weaving on the sides of Fig. 92.

Fig. 95. Coarse weaving of the inside of Fiji basketry.

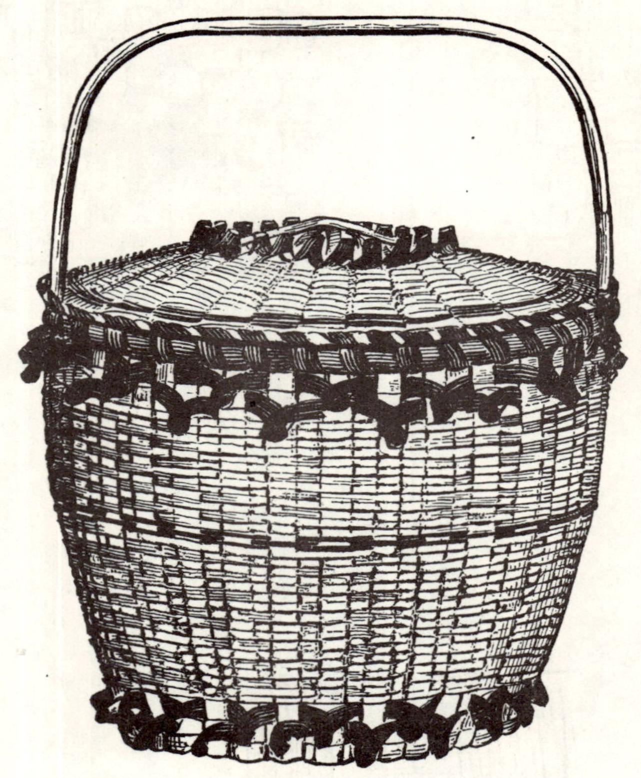

FIG. 96. Woven basket of Micmac Indians made of white birch. Thousands of these pretty baskets wrought into hundreds of shapes are sold in the towns and villages of the Northern States by the Indian basket-maker. A curious modification of this method of weaving comes from Tripoli, in which the horizontal part is rigid and the weft straws run up and down. It is as if we revolved the Micmac pattern 90 degrees. Collected by Mr. G. Brown Goode, in Nova Scotia.

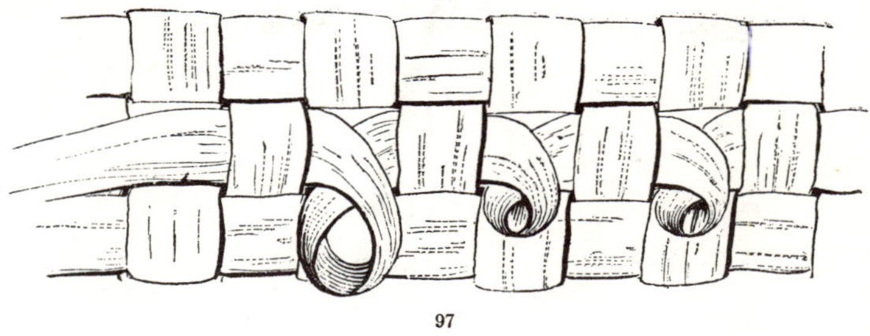

97

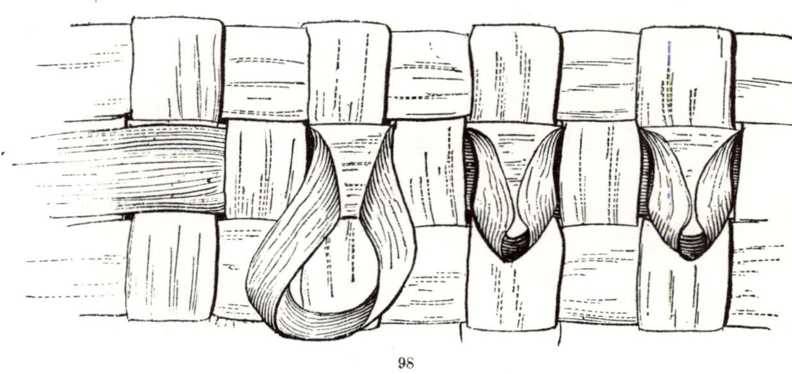

98

FIGS. 97, 98. Showing the method of introducing the curled ornament in Algonquin and Iroquois basketry.

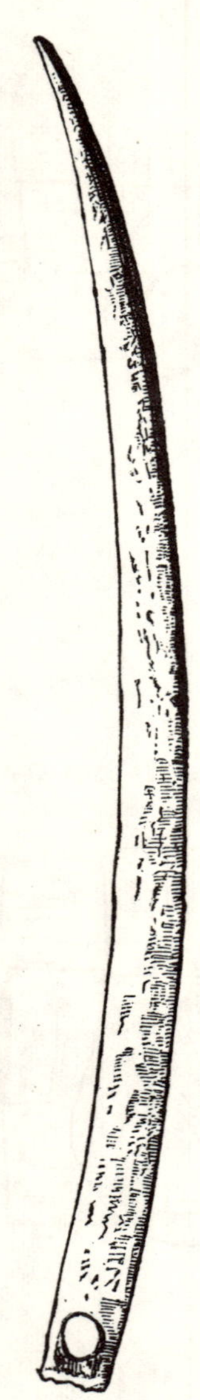

Fig. 99. Ordinary form of pricker used by Eskimo. Collected at Point Clarence

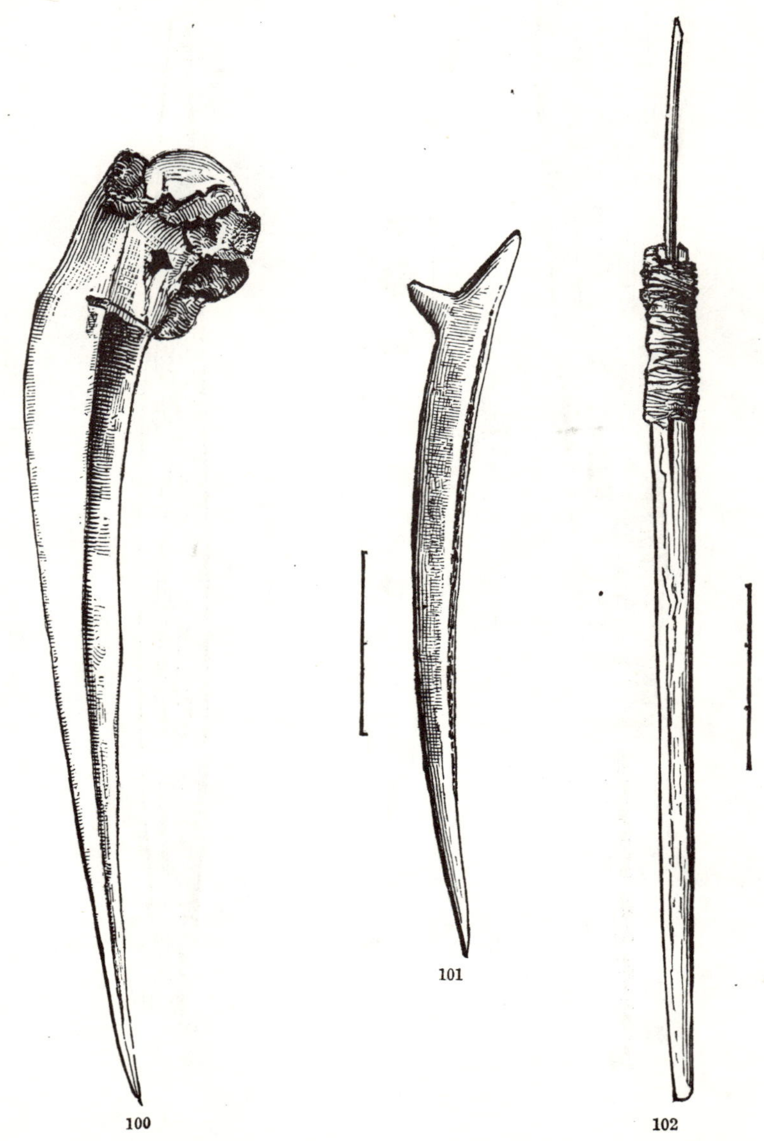

Figs. 100–102. Bone, ivory, and metal-pointed prickers from Lower Yukon district.

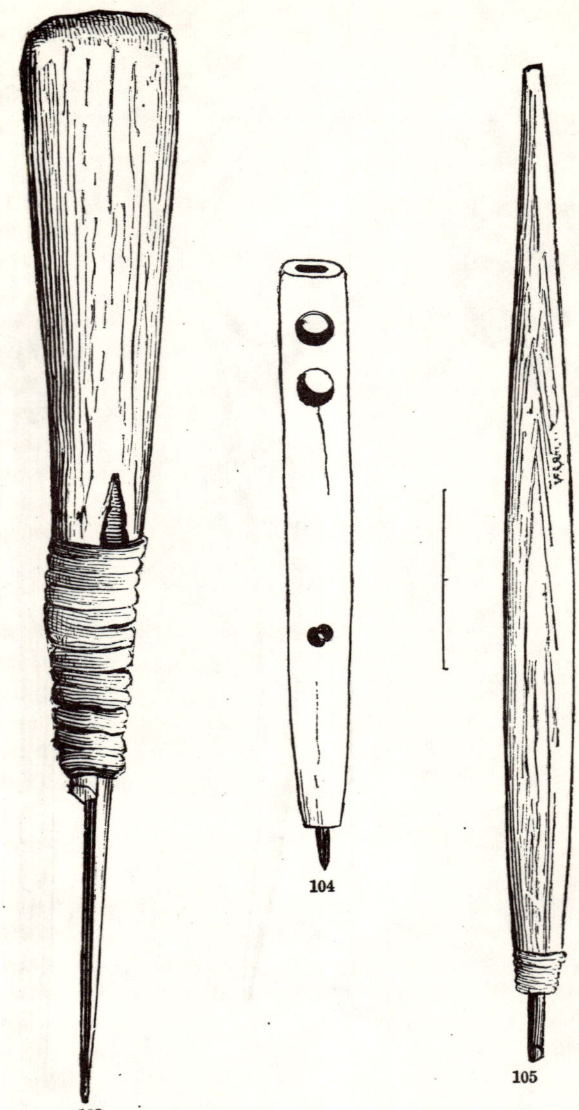

FIG. 103. Eskimo pricker with wooden handle and iron point lashed with rawhide.
FIG. 104. Eskimo awl, with metal point in ivory handle.
FIG. 105. Eskimo drill-shaft of wood with metal point and band of rawhide. Drills of this class also have beautiful jade points.

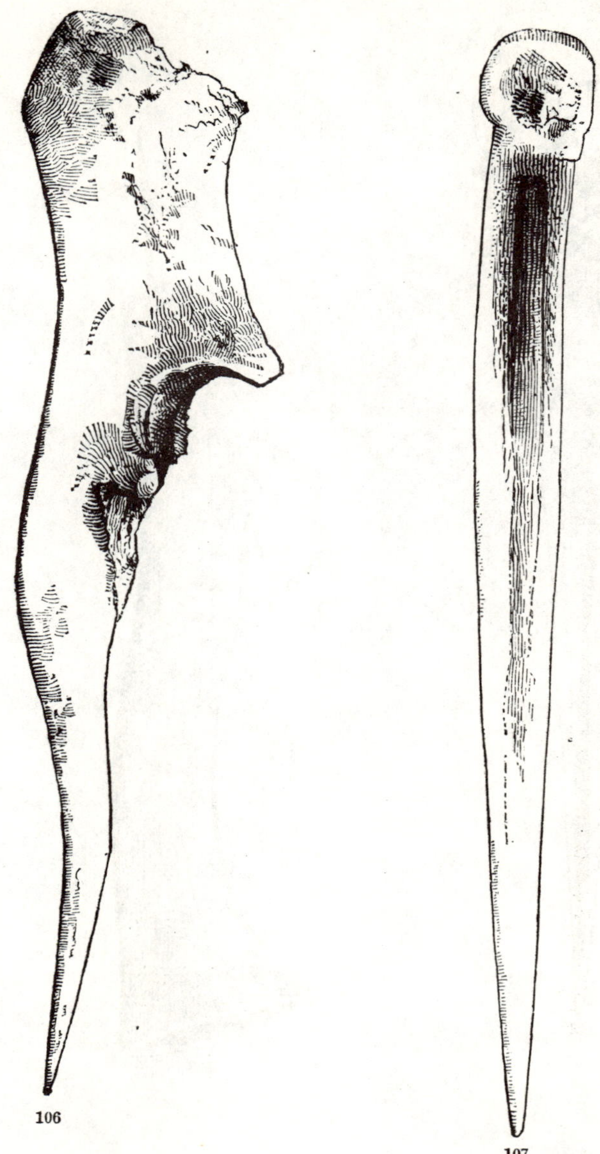

FIGS. 106, 107. Bone prickers used by Moquis. Collected in Arizona, by J. W. Powell.

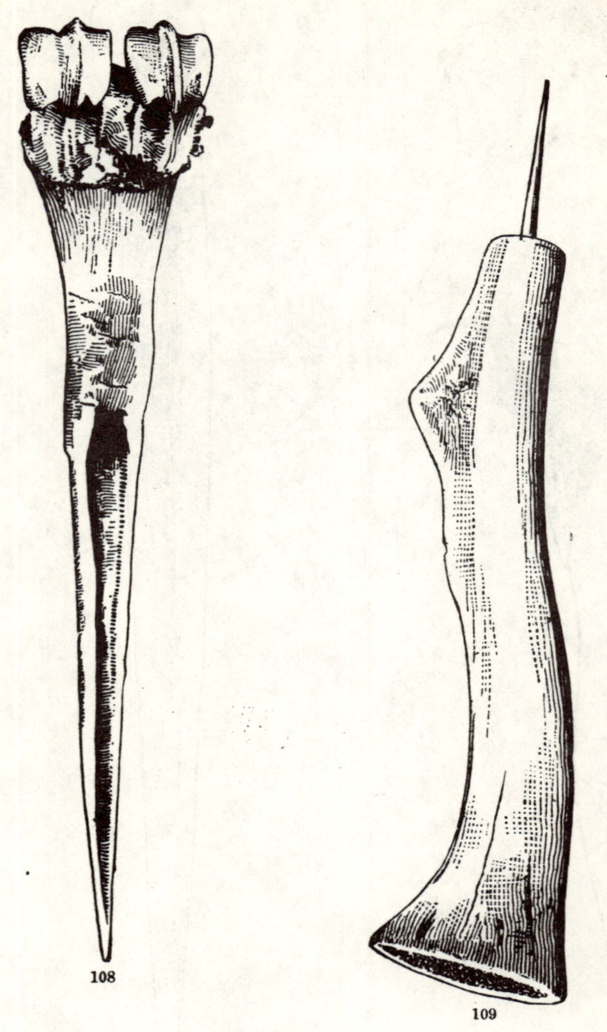

FIG. 108. Bone pricker from Coahuila, Mex. Collected by E. Palmer.
FIG. 109. Iron-pointed pricker of Cherokees. Collected in North Carolina, by E. Palmer.

A
Catalog Of
SHOREY PUBLICATIONS

SHOREY PUBLICATIONS IN PRINT

1. Glover, S.L. ORIGIN AND OCCURENCE OF GEM STONES IN WASHINGTON. 1949 — 1.00
2. Mooney, Jas. Ghost Dance Religion: SMOHALLA AND HIS DOCTRINE. 1896 — 1.50
3. Mooney. Ghost Dance Religion: SHAKERS OF PUGET SOUND. 1896 — 1.50
5. DICTIONARY OF CHINOOK JARGON. nd — 2.00
6. ALASKA RAILROAD TIME TABLES. 1922 — .50
7. Wells, E.H. UP AND DOWN THE YUKON. 1900 — 1.50
8. Williams, J.G. REPORT OF ATTORNEY GENERAL, Territory of Alaska, 1949-51. — 1.50
9. Gruening, Ernest. MESSAGE OF THE GOVERNOR OF ALASKA, 1946. — 2.00
10. Gruening. THIRD MESSAGE TO THE PEOPLE OF ALASKA, 1946. — 1.50
11. Kohlstedt, E.D. A GLIMPSE OF ALASKA. 1930 — 1.00
12. Gruening. MESSAGE OF THE GOVERNOR OF ALASKA, 1945. — 2.50
13. Leehey, M.D. PUBLIC LAND POLICY OF THE U.S. IN ALASKA. 1912 — 1.50
14. NOME TELEPHONE DIRECTORY. 1905 — 3.00
15. ESTABLISHMENT OF MT. MCKINLEY NATIONAL PARK. 1916 — 1.50
16. Hooper, Capt. C.L. CRUISE OF THE U.S. REVENUE STEAMER CORWIN IN ARCTIC OCEAN, November 1, 1880. — 7.50
17. Gruening. MESSAGE TO THE PEOPLE OF ALASKA. 1945 — 2.00
18. Gruening. MESSAGES OF THE GOVERNOR OF ALASKA. 1949 — 2.50
19. Davis, Geo. T. METLAKAHTLA. 1904 — 3.50
20. WORK OF THE BUREAU OF EDUCATION FOR NATIVES OF ALASKA. 1918 — 5.00
21. MacDowell, L.W. ALASKA INDIAN BASKETRY. — 1.00
22. Eells, Rev. Myron. THE TWANA, CHEMAKUM & KLALLAM INDIANS OF WASHINGTON TERRITORY. 1887 — 4.00
23. Grinnell, Joseph. GOLD HUNTING IN ALASKA. — 4.00
24. Swan, James G. INDIANS OF CAPE FLATTERY. — 7.50
25. CUSTER'S LAST BATTLE. 1892 — 2.00
26. Gruening, Sen. INDEPENDENCE DAY ADDRESS. 1959 — 1.75
27. Cadell, H.M. THE KLONDIKE AND YUKON GOLDFIELD IN 1913. 1914 — 2.50
28. Shiels, Archie W. EARLY VOYAGES OF THE PACIFIC. 1930 — 3.00
29. Fickett, E.D. METEOROLOGY. From Explorations in Alaska. 1900
30. Richardson, W.P. & others. YUKON RIVER EXPLORING EXPEDITION. Expl. in Alaska. 1900 — 2.00
31. Ray, P.H., W.P. Richardson. RELIEF OF THE DESTITUTE IN THE GOLDFIELDS. 1900 — 1.75
32. Shiels, Archie W. LITTLE JOURNEYS INTO THE HISTORY OF RUSSIAN AMERICA AND PURCHASE OF ALASKA. 1949 — 7.50
33. Shiels. STORY OF TWO DREAMS. 1957 — 4.00
34. Swan, J.G. HAIDAH INDIANS OF QUEEN CHARLOTTE'S ISLAND, B.C. 1874 — 5.00
35. Butler, Gen. B.V. & the Marquis of Lorne. THE BERING SEA CONTROVERSY. 1892 — 1.50
36. Crawford, Lewis F. THE MEDORA-DEADWOOD STAGE LINE. 1925 — 1.50
37. Anderson, Eskil. ASBESTOS AND JADE OCCURENCES IN KOBUK RIVER REGION, Alaska. 1945 — 2.00
38. Stewart, B.D. PROSPECTING IN ALASKA. 1949 — 1.50
39. Geoghegan, Richard H. THE ALEUT LANGUAGE. — 5.00
40. SEATTLE'S FIRST BUSINESS DIRECTORY. 1876 — 7.50
41. THE WASHBURN YELLOWSTONE EXPEDITION. 1871 — 1.25
42. Subreports from EXPLORATIONS IN ALASKA. 7 reports: The Tanana, Chickaloon, Sushitna, etc. 1900 — 2.00
43. Glenn, Capt. E.F. TANANA RIVER EXPLORING EXPEDITION. 1900 — 2.50
44. Glenn. COOK'S INLET EXPLORING EXPEDITION. 1900 — 1.75
45. WILKESON'S NOTES ON PUGET SOUND (1870?) — 2.50
46. (Perry). JOURNAL OF A VOYAGE TO THE ARCTIC REGIONS IN H.M.S. ALEXANDER, 1818. (1819?) — 6.00
47. BIENNIAL MESSAGE OF WM. M. BUNN, Governor of Idaho. 1884 — 2.00
48. MACKENZIE'S ROCK. Exploration of Sir Alexander Mackenzie. 1905 — 2.50
49. Williams, L.R. OUR PACIFIC COUNTY (Wash) — 5.00
50. AARON LADNER LINDSLEY..Founder of Alaska Missions. — 1.00
51. Evans, Elwood. PUGET SOUND: Its Past, Present and Future. 1869 — 2.50
52. Campbell, Robt. TWO JOURNALS, 1808-1853. — 15.00
53. Bernhardi, Madame Charlotte. MEMOIR OF THE CELEBRATED ADM. JOHN de KRUSENSTERN. 1856 — 5.00
54. McWhorter, Lucullus V. CRIME AGAINST THE YAKIMAS. 1931 — 4.50
55. Lupton, Chas T. OIL AND GAS IN THE OLYMPIC PENINSULA. 1913 — 4.00
56. Seward, Wm. H. THE ADMISSION OF KANSAS. A Speech. 1860 — 1.50
57. Stevens, Issac I. PROCLAMATION OF MARTIAL LAW. 1856 — .50
58. THE GLACIER - Tlinkit Training Academy, Vol. II. 1887 — .75
59. Hills, Rev. E.P. REV. AARON L. LINDSLEY. — .50
60. SWANTON'S HANDBOOK OF NORTH AMERICAN INDIANS, Pt. C: Indians of Alaska & Canada. 1952 — 5.00
61. Ward, D.B. ACROSS THE PLAINS IN 1853. 1911 — 3.50
62. MacDowell, Lloyd W. ALASKA TOTEM POLES. — 1.25
63. MacDowell. A TRIP TO WONDERFUL ALASKA. — 2.00
64. MacDowell. ALASKA GLACIERS & ICE FIELDS. — 1.25
65. Shaw, Geo. C. THE CHINOOK JARGON AND HOW TO USE IT. 1909 — 4.00

66. *PUGET SOUND COOPERATIVE COLONY. 1890's* 2.00
67. *THE HEROES OF BATTLE ROCK, or The Miners' Reward. 1904* 1.50
68. *Lampman, Ben Hur. CENTRALIA TRAGEDY AND TRIAL. 1920* 4.00
69. *SEAL FISHERY IN THE NORTH PACIFIC. (Correspondence with Russia.) 1895* 7.50
70. *Coolican, J.C. (ed.) PORT ANGELES. 1898* 4.00
71. *Jordan, D.S. TROUT AND SALMON OF THE PACIFIC COAST. 1906* 1.25
72. *COOPERATIVE PLAN FOR SECURING HOMES AT PORT ANGELES, Wash. 1893* 1.00
73. *Hidden, Maria L.T. OREGON PIONEERS. 1910* 1.00
74. *Stevens, Hazard. FIRST ASCENT OF TAKHOMA. Ext., 1876* 1.50
75. *DEMOCRATIC AND REPUBLICAN Ticket For Washington State and King County. 1889* .50
76. *THIRD ANNUAL COMMENCEMENT OF SEATTLE HIGH SCHOOL. 1888* .35
77. *ASSASSINATION OF PRESIDENT GARFIELD. Newspaper Extra. 1881?* .50
78. *PUGET SOUND CATECHISM. 1889* 1.00
79. *SEATTLE, KING COUNTY, WASHINGTON TERRITORY. Statistics & descriptive report. 1884* 1.50
80. *THE GREAT SEATTLE FIRE OF June 6, 1889.* 2.50
81. *USGS Bull. 442-D. MINING IN THE CHITINA DIST., etc. 1910* 2.50
82. *Swanton, John R. INDIAN TRIBES OF THE PACIFIC NORTHWEST. Ext., 1952* 6.00
83. *Sayre, Alex N. PUGET SOUND. Poem 1883* 1.50
84. *Bell, W.S. OLD FORT BENTON. 1909* 2.50
85. *Meany, Edmund S. INDIAN GEOGRAPHIC NAMES OF WASHINGTON. 1908* 1.00
86. *Swanton, J.R. INDIAN TRIBES OF AMERICAN SOUTHWEST. 1952* 6.00
87. *Swanton. INDIANS OF MEXICO, CENTRAL AMERICA AND WEST INDIES. 1952* 2.50
88. *USGS Bull. 836. SELECTED LIST OF USGS PUBLICATIONS ON ALASKA. 1930* 1.00
89. *Lewis, Wm. S. EARLY DAYS IN THE BIG BEND COUNTRY. 1926* 3.50
90. *Stoney, Geo. M. EXPLORATIONS IN ALASKA. 1899, Ext. from US Naval Inst.* 6.00
91. *Lindsley, A.L. SKETCHES OF AN EXCURSION TO SOUTHERN ALASKA. 1881* 5.00
92. *Collins, H.B. ARCHEOLOGY OF THE BERING SEA REGION. Ext., 1933* 1.50
93. *Ray and Murdoch. A VOCABULARY OF THE ESKIMOS OF POINT BARROW. 1885* 1.25
94. *Andrews, C.L. STORY OF SITKA. 1922* 5.00
95. *Matthews, Washington. NAVAJO WEAVERS. 1884* 2.50
96. *Dawson, Geo. M. THE HAIDAS. 1882* 1.00
97. *McClintock, Walter. FOUR DAYS IN A MEDICINE LODGE. 1900* 1.00
98. *Barbeau, Marius. MODERN GROWTH OF THE TOTEM POLES ON THE NORTHWEST COAST. 1939* 1.00
99. *SCRIPTURE SELECTIONS AND HYMNS IN HIDATSA or GROS VENTURE LANGUAGE. 1906* 1.50
100. *Baker, Marcus. GEOGRAPHIC DICTIONARY OF ALASKA. 1906* 3.00
101. *Lee, Charles A. ALEUTIAN INDIAN AND ENGLISH DICTIONARY. 1896* 1.00
102. *Shaw, Geo. C. VANCOUVER'S DISCOVERY OF PUGET SOUND IN 1792. 1933* 1.00
103. *Seward, Wm. H. SPEECHES in Alaska, Vancouver, and Oregon, 1869.* 2.50
104. *Rees, J.E. IDAHO: Chronology, Nomenclature, Biblio. 1918* 5.00
105. *Smith, W.C. THE EVERETT MASSACRE. 1916* 8.00
106. *PLACER MINING. 1897* 4.50
107. *Ross, Clyde P. THE VALDEZ CREEK MINING DISTRICT IN ALASKA. 1933* 5.00
108. *Stevens, Isaac I. TREATY BETWEEN THE U.S. AND THE DWAMISH, SUQUAMISH, & OTHER ALLIED AND SUBORDINATE TRIBES OF INDIANS IN WASHINGTON TERRITORY. 1855* 2.00
109. *Stevens, I.I. TREATY BETWEEN THE U.S. & THE NISQUALLY & OTHER BANDS OF INDIANS. 1855* 2.00
110. *Stevens. TREATY BETWEEN THE U.S. & THE YAKIMA NATION OF INDIANS. 1855* 2.00
111. *Stevens. TREATY BETWEEN THE U.S. OF A. & THE MAKAH TRIBE OF INDIANS. 1855* 2.00
112. *Stevens. TREATY BETWEEN THE U.S. AND THE INDIANS OF THE WILLAMETTE VALLEY. 1855* 2.00
113. *Densmore, F. STUDY OF INDIAN MUSIC. 1941* 1.50
114. *Harriman, Job. THE CLASS WAR IN IDAHO.* 3.00
115. *Ranck, G. PICTURES FROM NORTHWEST HISTORY.* 2.00
116. *Whitaker, R. OVERLAND TO OREGON. 1906* 4.00
117. *Krieger, H. INDIAN VILLAGES OF S.E. ALASKA.* 2.50
118. *Gatschet, A. THE KLAMATH INDIANS OF SOUTHWEST OREGON. 1890* 4.50
119. *Crane, W. TOTEM TALES. 1952* 4.00
120. *Bate, J. THE SECOND BOOKE TEACHING MOST PLAINLY AND COMPOSING OF ALL MANNER OF FIREWORKS FOR TRYUMPH AND RECREATION. 1635* 3.00
121. *James, G. PRACTICAL BASKET MAKING. 1917* 5.00
122. *Whorf, B. MAYA HIEROGLYPHS. 1941* 1.25
123. *Dall, Wm. MASKS, LABRETS, AND CERTAIN ABORIGINAL CUSTOMS. 1884* 8.50
124. *McCurdy, J. CAPE FLATTERY AND ITS LIGHT.* 1.00
125. *Wilhelm, Homer. THE SAN JUAN ISLANDS. 1901* 5.00
126. *Gaerity, Jack. BREAD AND ROSES FROM STONE.* 4.00
127. *Smith, W.C. WAS IT MURDER? (Centralia) 1922* 3.50
128. *HISTORY OF OWYHEE COUNTY. (Idaho)* 8.50
129. *Evans, Elwood. WASHINGTON TERRITORY. 1877* 3.00
130. *Delaney, Matilda Sagar. THE WHITMAN MASSACRE. 1920* 3.00
131. *Hubback, T.W. TEN THOUSAND MILES TO ALASKA FOR MOOSE AND SHEEP. 1921* 4.00
132. *Wilson, Katherine. COPPER-TINTS. 1923* 3.00
133. *Coleman, Edmund T. FIRST ASCENT OF MT. BAKER. Ext. from Harper's Monthly. 1869* 2.50
134. *Hodge, L.K. (ed.) MINING IN THE PACIFIC NORTHWEST. 1897* 30.00
134a. *Hodge. MINING IN WESTERN WASHINGTON. Ext from #134* 10.00

134b. Hodge. *MINING IN CENTRAL & EASTERN WASHINGTON.* Ext. from #134 10.00
134c. Hodge. *MINING IN SOUTHERN BRITISH COLUMBIA.* Ext. from #134 10.00
135. Stallard, Bruce. *ARCHEOLOGY IN WASHINGTON.* 1958 3.00
136. Lockley, Fred. *ALASKA'S FIRST FREE MAIL DELIVERY IN 1900.* 1.25
137. Strange. *JAMES STRANGE'S JOURNAL AND NARRATIVE OF THE COMMERCIAL EXPEDITION FROM BOMBAY TO THE NORTHWEST COAST OF AMERICA.* 1928 5.00
138. Hathaway, Ella C. *BATTLE OF THE BIG HOLE.* 2.00
139. Haller, Granville. *SAN JUAN & SECESSION.* 1.50
140. *THE KLONDIKE NEWS.* Vol. 1 #1, Dawson Newspaper. 1898 (Alaska's rarest newspaper) 10.00
141. *JOURNAL OF MEDOREM CRAWFORD.* 1897 2.00
142. *OCOSTA! The Ocean Terminus of the Northern Pacific R.R. and Coast City of Washington.* 2.50
143. Sutherland, T.A. *HOWARD'S CAMPAIGN AGAINST THE NEZ PERCE INDIANS, 1877.* 1878 3.50
144. Matthews, Mathew. *THE CATLIN COLLECTION OF INDIAN PAINTINGS.* 1890 3.00
145. Lockley, Fred. *TO OREGON BY OX TEAM IN '47.* 1.25
146. Lockley. *VIGILANTE DAYS IN VIRGINIA CITY.* 1.50
147. Judson, Katherine. *MYTHS AND LEGENDS OF THE PACIFIC NORTHWEST.* 1910 7.50
148. Whiting, Dr. F.B. *GRIT, GRIEF AND GOLD.* 10.00
149. Amundsen, Capt. Roald. *TO THE NORTH MAGNETIC POLE AND THROUGH THE NORTHWEST PASSAGE.* 3.00
150. Butte Businessmen's Assn. *BUTTE, MONTANA.* 2.00
151. Immigration Aid Society of Washington Terr. *NORTHWESTERN WASHINGTON.* 1880 3.50
152. Denig, Edwin T. *INDIAN TRIBES OF THE UPPER MISSOURI.* 1930 10.00
153. Buckley, Rev. J.M. *TWO WEEKS IN THE YOSEMITE AND VICINITY.* 1888 2.50
154. *SPEECH OF THE HON. R.C. WINTHROP OF MASS. ON THE PRESIDENT'S MESSAGE (on admission of California)* 1850 2.00
155. Marshall, Martha. *A PRONOUNCING DICTIONARY OF CALIFORNIA NAMES IN ENGLISH AND SPANISH.* 2.50
156. Mercer, A.S. *BIG HORN COUNTY, WYOMING.* 7.50
157. Moorehead, Warren K. *PREHISTORIC RELICS.* 7.50
158. Merrill, Geo. P. *NOTES ON THE GEOLOGY AND NATURAL HISTORY OF THE PENINSULA OF LOWER CALIFORNIA.* 1895 2.00
159. Georgeson, C.C. *REINDEER & CARIBOU.* 1904 1.50
160. Hewett, Edgar L. *A GENERAL VIEW OF THE ARCHEOLOGY OF THE PUEBLO REGION.* 1904 2.00
161. Bennett, Wm. P. *THE FIRST BABY IN CAMP.* 3.50
162. Coffman, Noah B. *OLD LEWIS COUNTY, Oregon Territory.* 1926 3.50
163. Bebbe, Mrs. Iola. *THE TRUE LIFE STORY OF SWIFTWATER BILL GATES.* 1908 7.50
164. Costello. *THE SIWASH - THEIR LIFE, LEGENDS AND TALES.* 1895 10.00
165. Murie, Olaus J. *ALASKA-YUKON CARIBOU.* 10.00
166. Meeker, Ezra. *STORY OF THE LOST TRAIL TO OREGON, NO. 2.* 1916 2.50
167. Hanna, Rev. J.A. *DR. WHITMAN AND HIS RIDE TO SAVE OREGON.* 1903 1.25
168. Hadwen, Seymore & Laurence J. Palmer. *REINDEER IN ALASKA.* 1922 5.00
169. Geer, T.T. *THE ROMANCE OF ASTORIA.* 1911 1.75
170. Williams, Lewis. *CHINOOK BY THE SEA.* 7.50
171. *SAN FERNANDO VALLEY.* 1938 2.00
172. *PASADENA.* 1938 2.00
173. Ingalls, Maj. J.W. *HISTORY OF WASHOE COUNTY, NEVADA.* 1913 5.00
174. Reid, J.T. & J.R. Hunter. *HUMBOLT COUNTY.* 1913 4.50
175. Aston. *ESMERALDA COUNTY.* 1913 4.50
176. London, Jack. *THE GOLD HUNTERS OF THE NORTH.* Ext., 1903. 1.25
177. Wartman-Arland, Flora E. *THE STORY OF MONTESANO.* 1933 4.00
178. London. *THE ECONOMICS OF THE KLONDIKE.* 1.50
179. Bishop, Robert Sr. *LAND IN THE SKY TOTEM.* 1.50
180. Webb, John S. & Ed S. Curtis. *THE RIVER TRIP TO THE KLONDIKE AND THE RUSH TO THE KLONDIKE OVER THE MOUNTAIN PASS.* 1898 2.50
181. Librn. of Bellingham Public Libr. *HISTORY OF BELLINGHAM.* 1926 6.00
182. *VOYAGE OF ALEXANDER MACKENZIE.* 2.50
183. Chaplin, Ralph. *CENTRALIA CONSPIRACY.* 4.50
184. Haswell, Robert. *ROBERT HASWELL'S JOURNALS.* 1788-89. 4.00
185. Minto, John. *RHYME OF EARLY LIFE IN OREGON.* (1915?) 4.00
186. Collins, Henry B., A.H. Clarke & E.H. Walker. *THE ALEUTIAN ISLANDS: Their People & Natural History.* 1945 7.50
187. Simpson, Brevet Brig. Gen. J.H. *CORONADO'S MARCH IN SEARCH OF THE "SEVEN CITIES OF CIBOLA."* 1871 2.50
188. Riddle, Geo. W. *EARLY DAYS IN OREGON.* 5.00
189. *VILHJALMUR STEFANSON.* 1925 2.50
190. Lockley, Fred. *ACROSS THE PLAINS BY PRAIRIE SCHOONER.* 1.50
191. MacArthur, Walter. *LAST DAYS OF SAIL ON THE WEST COAST.* 1929 7.50
192. Stuck, Hudson. *T E ALASKAN MISSIONS OF THE EPISCOPAL CHURCH.* 1920 10.00
193. Steffa, Don. *TALES OF NOTED FRONTIER CHARACTERS, SOAPY SMITH.* 1908 1.75.
194. Meeker, E. *WASGUBGTIB TERRUTIRT, k870* 3.00
195. Denny, Arthur A. *PIONEER DAYS ON PUGET SOUND.* 1888 5.00
196. Rowan, James. *THE I.W.W. IN THE LUMBER INDUSTRY.* 4.00
199. Sayre, J. Willis. *THE EARLY WATERFRONT OF SEATTLE, 1937.* 2.50

204. Pelly, T.M. DR. MINOR - A SKEtch of His Background and Life. 1933 7.50
209. Flandrau, Grace. FRONTIER DAYS ALONG THE UPPER MISSOURI. 3.00
210. Flandrau. THE LEWIS AND CLARK EXPEDITION. 5.00
211. Flandrau. A GLANCE AT THE LEWIS AND CLARK EXPEDITION. 3.00
213. Flandrau. THE VERENDRYE OVERLAND QUEST OF THE PACIFIC. 3.50
216. Harper, Frank B. FORT UNION AND ITS NEIGHBORS ON THE UPPER MISSOURI. 2.50
220. Burdick, Usher L. MARQUIS de MORES AT WAR IN THE BADLANDS. 1929 2.50
227. General Strike Committee. THE SEATTLE GENERAL STRIKE. 1919 5.00
231. Sayre, J.W. THE ROMANCE OF SECOND AVENUE. 1.50
235. DEDICATION AND OPENING OF THE NEW CASCADE TUNNEL. 1929 2.00
239. Van Olinda, O.S. HISTORY OF VASHON - MAURY ISLAND. 1935 6.00
241. Hanford, C.H. SAN JUAN DISPUTE. 1900 2.00
246. Walgamott, C.S. REMINISCENCES OF EARLY DAYS. 1926 7.50
250. Wardner, Jim. JIM WARDNER, OF WARDNER IDAHO. 1900 8.00
251. Brown, Col. W.C. THE SHEEPEATER CAMPAIGN, Idaho - 1879. 1926 2.50
259. Hornaday, Wm. T. EXTERMINATION OF THE AMERICAN BISON. 1887? 10.00
264. Slauson, Morda C. ONE HUNDRED YEARS ON THE CEDAR. 10.00
265. Jones, S.C. & M.F. Casady. FROM CABIN TO CUPOLA. County Courthouses in Washington. 10.00
267. Andrews, Clarence L. WRANGELL AND THE GOLD OF THE CASSIAR. 1937 3.50
268. Andrews, Clarence L. THE PIONEERS AND THE NUGGETS OF VERSE. 1937 3.00
280. PORT TOWNSEND. 1890 5.00
281. Gilbert, Kenneth. ALASKAN POKER STORIES. 1958 2.50
282. Moore, James Bernard. SKAGWAY IN DAYS PRIMEVAL. 4.00
283. Chase, Cora G. UNTO THE LEAST. 1972 6.00
284. Blankenship, Geo. E. EARLY HISTORY OF THURSTON COUNTY. 1914 20.00
285. Fish, Harriet U. PAST AT PRESENT. 1967 12.50
286. Allen, Edward W. THE ROLLICKING PACIFIC; A Selection of Poems. 1972 3.00
287. Allen. DANCING TALES. 1951 4.00

SJU 1. Farlow, Dr. W.G. SOME EDIBLE AND POISONOUS FUNGI. 1897 2.50
SJU 2. Gurdji, V. ORIENTAL RUG WEAVING. 1901 5.00
SJU 3. D'Avenes, E., Prisse & Dr. J.C. Ewart. EGYPTIAN AND ARABIAN HORSES AND ORIGIN OF HORSES AND PONIES. 1904 2.50
SJU 4. Freshfield, Douglas W. ON MOUNTAINS AND MANKIND. 1904 1.50
SJU 5. Davenport, Cyril. CAMEOS. 1904 1.50
SJU 6. Maire, Albert. MATERIALS USED TO WRITE UPON BEFORE THE INVENTION OF PRINTING. 1.50
SJU 7. Liberty, Arthur L. PEWTER AND THE REVIVAL OF ITS USE. 1904 1.50
SJU 8. Hammell, Wm. PINE NEEDLE BASKETRY. 1.50
SJU 9. Frey, Clark, Vietch. HOME TANNING. 1936 1.50
SJU 10. Browning, Frank. STEAM PLANT ERRORS 2.00
SJU 18. Burdick, Arthur J. THE PROSPECTOR'S MANUAL. 1905 7.50
SJU 19. WOODS DUAL POWER. (1902?) 1.50
SJU 20. Hayward, Charles B. DIRIGIBLE BALLOONS. 1921 5.00
SJU 21. Osborn, Henry F. THE ELEPHANTS AND MASTEDONS ARRIVE IN AMERICA 1.50
SJU 22. Todd, Mattie Phipps. HAND LOOM WEAVING. 1902 7.00
SJU 23. Wilbur, C. Martin. HISTORY OF THE CROSSBOW. 1936 1.50
SJU 24. Alexander, A.S. HORSE SECRETS. 1913 2.50
SJU 26. Clute, Willard Nelson. THE FERN - COLLECTOR'S GUIDE. 1901 3.00
SJU 27. Meeker, E. HOP CULTURE IN THE U.S. 1883 10.00

SJI 1. Krause, F. SLING CONTRIVANCES. 1904 2.00
SJI 2. Murdoch, John. A STUDY OF THE ESKIMO BOWS IN THE U.S. NATIONAL MUSEUM. 1884 1.50
SJI 3. Mason, Otis T. THROWING STICKS IN THE NATIONAL MUSEUM. 1884. 2.50
SJI 4. CHIEF JOSEPH'S OWN STORY. 1879 2.50
SJI 5. Mason, Otis. BASKET WORK OF THE ABORIGINES. 1884 5.00
SJI 6. Llwd, Rev. Dr. J.P.D. THE MESSAGE OF AN INDIAN RELIC: Seattle's Totem Pole. 2.00
SJI 7. Mason, O. TRAPS OF THE AMERICAN INDIAN. 1.25
SJI 8. Meeker, Louis L. OGALALA GAMES. 1901 1.50
SJI 9. Collins, Henry B. PREHISTORIC ART OF THE ALASKAN ESKIMO. 1929 3.50
SJI 10. Eells, Rev. M. JUSTICE TO THE INDIAN. 1.00
SJI 11. Willoughby, C. INDIANS OF THE QUINAIELT AGENCY, Washington Territory. 1886 1.50
SJI 12. Leon & Holmes. STUDIES ON THE ARCHAEOLOGY OF MICHOACAN MEXICO... 1886 2.00
SJI 13. Beckwith, Paul. NOTES ON CUSTOMS OF THE DAKOTAHS. 1886 1.25
SJI 14. Eells, Rev. M. THE STONE AGE. 1886 1.50
SJI 15. Allen, Lt. Henry T. ATNATANAS NATIVES OF COPPER RIVER, ALASKA. 1886 1.00
SJI 16. Yates, Dr. L.G. CHARM STONES. 1886 1.50
SJI 17. Boas, Fran . THE CENTRAL ESKIMO. 1884 12.50
SJI 18. Gibbs, Geo. & others. TRIBES OF THE EXTREME NORTHWEST, ALASKA, THE ALEUTIANS AND ADJACENT TERRITORIES. Ext. 1877 15.00
SJI 19. Gibbs & others. LANGUAGES OF THE TRIBES OF THE EXTREME NORTHWEST, ALASKA, THE ALEUTIANS AND ADJACENT TERRITORY. 6.00

SJI 20. Gibbs, Geo., Dr. Wm. F. Tolmie, & Father G. Mengarini. TRIBES OF WESTERN WASHINGTON AND NORTHWESTERN OREGON. 20.00

SJI 21. Gibbs, Geo & others. COMPARATIVE VOCABULARIES OF THE TRIBES OF WESTERN WASHINGTON AND NORTHWESTERN OREGON. part of SJI 20. 5.00

SJI 22. Gibbs, Geo. A DICTIONARY OF THE NISQUALLY INDIAN LANGUAGE. part of SJI 20. 10.00

SJI 23. Boas, Franz. INTRODUCTION TO HANDBOOK OF AMERICAN INDIAN LANGUAGES. Ext. 1911 5.00

SJI 24. Swanton, John R. THE TLINGIT INDIAN LANGUAGE. From Hndbk. of Amer. Indian Lang. 3.00

SJI 25. Swanton. THE HAIDA INDIAN LANGUAGE. 5.00

SJI 26. Boas. THE TSIMSHIAN INDIAN LANGUAGE. 8.00

SJI 27. Boas. THE KWAKIUTL INDIAN LANGUAGE. 7.50

SJI 28. Boas. THE CHINOOK INDIAN LANGUAGE. 5.00

SJI 29. Boas & Swanton. THE SIOUAN, Dakota INDIAN LANGUAGE. 6.00

SJI 30. Talbitzer, Wm. THE ESKIMO LANGUAGE. 6.50

SJI 31. Ewers, John C. EARLY WHITE INFLUENCE UPON PLAINS INDIAN PAINTING. 1957 2.00

SJI 32. Fenton, Wm. N. CONTRACTS BETWEEN IROQUOIS HERBALISM AND COLONIAL MEDICINE. 1941 2.00

SJI 38. Remington, Fred. ARTIST WANDERINGS AMONG THE CHEYENNES. 1889 1.50

SJI 41. Bagley, Clarence. INDIAN MYTHS OF THE NORTHWEST. 1930 8.50

SJI 43. Mason, O. ABORIGINAL SKIN DRESSING. 5.00

SJI 46. Thorne, J. Frederic. IN THE TIME THAT WAS. 1909 2.50

SJI 49. DeSmet, Rev. P.J. NEW INDIAN SKETCHES. 8.50

SJI 51. Mason, O. MAN'S KNIFE AMONG THE NORTH AMERICAN INDIANS. 1899 2.00

SJI 53. Holmes, William H. POTTERY OF THE ANCIENT PUEBLOS. 1886 6.00

SJI 55. Dorsey, James O. A STUDY OF SIOUAN CULTS 1894 10.00

SJI 57. Mason, O. POINTED BARK CANOES OF THE KUTENAI AND AMUR. 1901 2.00

SJI 58. Mason, O. ABORIGINAL AMERICAN HARPOONS. 1902 7.50

SJI 59. Hough, Walter. THE LAMP OF THE ESKIMO. 1898 5.00

SJI 61. Drucker, Philip. ARCHAEOLOGICAL SURVEY CN THE NORTHERN NORTHWEST COAST. 1943. 7.00

SJI 62. INDIANS IN WASHINGTON. 3.00

NOTE TO STUDENTS AND COLLECTORS

Many scarce items turn up in antiquarian book stores only once. And while such works are in great demand, the high prices usually commanded by the older, scarcer items put them beyond the reach of the average student and the small collector. To meet this need we are bringing back into print a diversity of Pacific Northwest and Alaskan historical material which we are selling at moderate prices. In their original form these bring prices ranging from $3.00 to $100.00; some even higher.

We limit most reproductions from 25 to 100 copies and reprint as the demand warrants. The books have heavy paper covers. They show both original and reprinting dates. Regular library and dealer discounts granted. For detailed descriptions of these titles send for Shorey's Catalog of Publications #3. It also lists future Shorey Publications.